Essentials of
Public Relations
Management

Essentials of Public Relations Management

Edward J. Lordan, Ph.D.
West Chester University

Burnham Inc., Publishers

Chicago

President: Kathleen Kusta
Vice-President: Brett J. Hallongren
Project Editors: Nancy Banaszak and Sheila Whalen
Design/Production: Tamra Phelps
Cover Illustration: "People in Ear," Ken Orvidas, © 2002 Getty Images
Printer: Cushing-Malloy, Inc.

Material used on pages 7, 10, 14, 18, 21, 25, 29, 30, 31, 33, 34, 35, 48, 51, 59, 60, 61, 63, 67, 77, 93, 96, 105, 147, 155 courtesy of Public Relations Tactics. Copyright by Public Relations Tactics. Reprinted with permission from PRSA <www.prsa.org>.

Library of Congress Cataloging-in-Publication Data
Lordan, Edward J.
  Essentials of public relations management / Edward J. Lordan.
    p. cm.
  ISBN 0-8304-1594-7 (pbk)
  1. Public relations—Management. I. Title.
  HD59 .L67 2001
  659.2—dc21
                              2002004398

Manufactured in the United States of America

10 9 8 7 6 5 4 3 2 1

The paper used in this book meets the minimum requirements of American National Standard for Information Sciences—Permanence of Paper for Printed Library Materials, ANSI Z39.48-1984.

To my loving wife

Mary Elizabeth Chollet Lordan

and my two sons

Daniel and Brendan

Contents

Introduction

You are the one who can stretch your own horizon ...
—Edgar F. Magnin

Why a book about public relations management? Consider a common career trajectory for the public relations (PR) practitioner and a common observation about the status of public relations in an organization.

First, the traditional career trajectory. Many people in the public relations industry gravitate toward the field long before they are even aware it exists. In high school, they are the students organizing homecomings and volunteering for community fund-raisers. In college, many choose majors in English, journalism, or general communications; others concentrate on sociology, psychology, or marketing. They are often avid readers who like to interact and exchange ideas.

In a typical internship or first job, the PR practitioner learns the basics by clipping articles, organizing files, updating media lists. If all goes well, this work leads to writing assignments and media contact opportunities. The practitioner becomes more news-savvy, honing writing skills and media relations techniques. Experience and growing confidence result in increased direct interaction with clients, perhaps leading to opportunities to pitch new business.

Unfortunately, this is where many public relations careers "top out." The experience and knowledge developed in a traditional PR career prepare many practitioners to achieve merely mid-level positions rather than positions as managers. Meanwhile, people with managerial skills who have advanced along different career tracks continue to move up.

This book is designed to help practitioners who have moved along a traditional track to advance into management. While this text focuses extensively on the micro or intra-agency level, it also addresses management from the macro level, or client side. Understanding the perspectives of both the consumer and the producer of public relations services is a critical to developing management skills.

The text is also designed to help raise the profile of public relations in general. Public relations practitioners often feel that they are not given adequate recognition by management—that public relations is not perceived to have sufficient gravitas to justify a management position. This attitude is reflected in the literature of public relations; textbooks, research journals, and professional publications invariably report that the industry "continues to work with the highest levels of management" to "get a place at the table where decisions are made." The fact that assurances are still being made suggests that public relations has not made much progress in getting that place. This book, then, is also designed to help people in public relations develop the tools to function as managers of public relations departments, and learn to think as managers of organizations in general— to help members of the profession really get that "seat at the management table."

The book is divided into chapters designed to explain the theory, techniques, and priorities of management. Chapters on personnel, finance, legal, and technology issues introduce these key management areas. Boxed materials provide perspectives and lessons from professionals in the business. An action plan at the end of each chapter provides an opportunity to apply the essential lessons from each chapter.

This book is only one component in the development of a public relations career. There are many other factors—working with a strong mentor, strategic networking, and, of course, plain old hard work—that are essential to career development. The PR professional who aspires to a management position commits to continued professional development.

I would like to acknowledge the contributions of a number of people who have helped in the development of this text. These include public relations researchers such as James Grunig, William Ehling, and Robert Heath, who have edited and contributed to a number of important public relations texts referenced in this book. My colleagues Jim Marra, Tom Eveslage, and Ed Trayes at Temple University have been extremely supportive: Jim reviewed and provided extremely useful input to the original book proposal; Tom was extremely helpful in reviewing the legal chapter; and Ed has been of invaluable assistance on this and other projects. Professor Dennis Klinzing, chair of the Department of Communication Studies at West Chester University, has been extremely encouraging throughout the process of writing this text. I would also like to acknowledge the assistance of three members of the Burnham, Inc., Publishers team: Production/Design Manager Tamra Phelps, for keeping the book on schedule and creating the clarity of the layout; and editors Nancy Banaszak and Sheila Whalen, for significantly improving the quality of the writing.

Finally, my wife and first reader, Mary Elizabeth Chollet Lordan, spent countless hours proofing these pages and improving my writing. When she wasn't doing that or a thousand other things, she was caring for our two sons, Daniel and Brendan, while I was tapping away on the computer. I dedicate this book to the three of them, and thank them for the sacrifices they made while I wrote it.

CHAPTER 1

Client Relations

Coming together is a beginning; Keeping together is progress;
Working together is success.
—Henry Ford

This chapter focuses on the relationship between public
relations managers and their clients. It discusses the
unique qualities of these critical relationships, explores
the traditional roles that evolve between clients and PR managers,
and details strategies a manager can use to improve the relationship so that both parties derive maximum benefits from it.

Demonstrating Value, Developing Trust

The customer/vendor relationship in many businesses is relatively
simple. In manufacturing, for example, it can be based on a transac-
tion as simple as the delivery of X widgets for Y dollars.

In public relations, however, the relationship between customer
(client) and vendor (public relations manager) is far more complex.
From the beginning, trust—not transactions—underpins the success of the partnership; a PR manager's effectiveness depends on
access to the organization's most sensitive information. Furthermore,
the value of public relations is usually more subjective than the value
of other goods and services. The client may have no experience in

1.1: The Economic Case for Public Relations

Your bottom-line client thinks only in terms of the cost/benefit ratio—an equation that puts you at a disadvantage, right?

Wrong. Not only is it possible to evaluate public relations activity on a cost/benefit basis, it is advantageous to do so. PR researcher William Ehling points out that:

> Public relations is not subject to rigorous benefits-cost analysis because management reduces public relations to low-level communication production activities which are treated simply as a "cost of doing business." Communications and public relations activities are viewed as generating no direct tangible benefits to the organization as a whole .... Such management conceptualizations of public relations (specifically, of the tasks and responsibilities assigned this activity) reflect a lack of sustained organizational commitment to public relations as a strategic management function. This lack of commitment, coupled with conceptual flaws, deflect both public relations practitioners and top-level executives from focusing serious attention on the economic importance of public relations and on its benefit-cost relationship.*

M.S. Thompson suggests an eight-step process for conducting a cost-benefit analysis of public relations activities:

1. Identify the decision-makers and their basic concerns.
2. Identify alternative programs of action available to the decision-makers.
3. Identify costs, including program expenses and all unwelcome disbenefits.
4. Identify benefits, including both direct and indirect benefits.
5. Assign monetary values to the program's effects.

6. Discount if effects occur at different times (if all effects occur at the same time, discounting is not needed.)
7. Take into account, when appropriate, the distributional equity effects.
8. Aggregate and interpret the resultant variant effects.[†]

The cost-benefit analysis is an important, trusted technique for many managers, so it is an approach the PR manager should use as well. Assigning economic value to services and outcomes can be more complicated in public relations than it is in other areas, but doing so allows you to frame your contributions in a form that is understood, and appreciated, by management.

[*]Ehling, William P., "Estimating the Value of Public Relations and Communication to an Organization," in *Excellence in Public Relations and Communication Management*, ed. Grunig, 620.

[†]Thompson, M.S., *Benefit-Cost Analysis for Program Evaluation*, (Beverly Hills, CA: Sage, 1980).

public relations and may even be suspicious of the terms, strategies, and goals of such a program. New clients may not understand the advantages and disadvantages, opportunities and limitations of public relations.

At the end of the month, when a client reviews his accounts, he will pick up his first invoice and note that one supplier has billed him Y dollars and has provided him with X widgets—physical goods that he can see in his plant. He will pick up a second invoice, a bill for public relations services, and he will look around and see . . . what?

This is why the PR manager must understand and remain constantly conscious of the client/vendor relationship. Client concerns about the value of public relations are as valid as concerns about the productivity of any other cost center. Unfortunately, PR consultants often fall short when answering questions about the end product. As veteran PR researcher William Ehling wrote, "Outlays for public relations activities beg an obvious managerial question: What is being accomplished in monetary terms? Answers to this question are generally muted, murky, and often misleading."[1]

To be effective and keep customers happy, public relations managers must *educate* as they *sell*. In fact, managers should maintain a regular education program to ensure that their customers remain aware of the value of their services.

An Evolutionary Role

In most customer/vendor relationships in public relations, the managers' roles evolve over time, as their clients become more familiar with, and dependent upon, their advice. Nager and Truitt note that:

> A partnership depends on trust. Trust depends upon openness of communication and sensitivity to another's interests. That sensitivity depends upon taking pains to discover and verify those interests and keep them in mind. Discovery and verification are based upon astute questioning, observation, and listening. Strategic listening requires that the prospective client partner will be willing to talk. This willingness to open up depends, again, upon trust.[2]

In building this trust, managers must be continually aware of the evolutionary nature of their role. Savvy managers will help guide this evolution by familiarizing themselves with their clients' organizations and industries while consistently working to provide higher, more management-oriented levels of service as the relationship progresses.

While no two manager/client relationships are identical, there are some traditional roles. Broom and Smith hypothesize five models to describe the relationship and expectations between public relations consultants and their clients.[3] While the authors do not suggest a direct progression or hierarchy of roles, they do note that it is common for the relationships to move from a technical, project-oriented basis to a more general, advisory role. They also note that each of the following roles offers advantages and disadvantages to both parties. The five roles:

Technical Services Provider

> The practitioner is hired for communication skills and mass media experience. . . . Other specialized services "purchased" by clients include graphics, photography, publication and broadcast production, public opinion research, special events planning, fund raising, exhibit planning, and production.[4]

This relationship has significant limitations because the PR manager may not gain access to key constituents or necessary information.

Communication Process Facilitator

In this role, the practitioner functions as an information mediator among decision-making parties. "The consultant in this role is most concerned with maintaining full participation of those involved and maximum information exchange."[5] The role assumes that the consultant will make the best contribution by working to provide relevant information to key decision-makers to produce the best strategic decisions.

Problem-Solving Process Facilitator

This role involves a "collaborative relationship in which the consultant helps the client apply a systematic problem-solving approach."[6] Again, the consultant is operating as a facilitator, assisting in the decision-making process. Key contributions in this role have less to do with introducing fresh approaches than with helping to draw the best information from important constituents within the organization.

Acceptant
Legitimizer

In this role, the public relations manager, functioning as an outside, independent evaluator, reinforces a set of existing concepts by restating them. The primary contribution of this supportive role is to provide an external seal of approval to a direction that management has already agreed on. Managers in this position rarely contribute new ideas to an organization.

Expert
Prescriber

In this most powerful role, the consultant "operates *as an authority* [emphasis added in the original] on both the public relations problem and the solution that should be implemented."[7] While the expert prescriber might seem to be the ideal position, it also carries both advantages and disadvantages. The client may come to depend on the consultant for input on a range of issues beyond the scope of public relations. While such a "guru role" can be flattering and lucrative, it can also be risky. There is also a danger that public relations will be viewed as an autonomous function, ignoring the interdependence between public relations and other departments in the organization.

Sometimes the role of the PR manager will be narrowly defined and won't deviate much from the initial relationship. More often, however, the manager's power will wax and wane in an organization, depending on a wide range of factors. A client may initially be seeking technical services—for example, writing, packaging information, or addressing a one-time need. Gradually, the manager may be called on—or volunteer—for more management-oriented tasks, as described in Broom and Smith's models.

Ultimately, PR managers are responsible for helping shape their relationships in the ways that allow them to contribute most effectively to their clients' organizations.

Strategic Contributions

How can the manager influence the relationship? That depends where the manager wants the relationship to go.

The PR manager lays the foundation for influencing the relationship by providing strong, dependable service, meeting the client's specific needs, and gradually earning the client's confidence. To better understand the client's needs, the PR manager needs to learn as much as possible about the organization and its industry. CEOs consistently identify a thorough knowledge of the organization's business as the most essential qualification for PR professionals, according to PR author Carole M. Howard.

> Top executives and other decision makers will find it difficult to take advice from anyone who does not have a thorough understanding of the business. It's essential that you constantly update your knowledge of the organization you represent, its strategy, its position in the marketplace, its growth and expansion plans.[8]

At the micro level, the manager should become as familiar as possible with the organization's business and marketing plans and talk with as many key decision-makers as possible. This process will be most successful if it progresses at a comfortable pace for the client, since it involves sharing critical information. At the macro level, the manager should talk to competitors, join professional associations related to the industry, read the industry trade press (including Web sites), and identify and create relationships with members of the press who cover the organization and industry.

Once the manager truly knows the territory, the next step is to use this information to develop meaningful recommendations for management. It is essential to synthesize the key issues and trends that affect the client's industry—to "see around the corner" to help the client react to today's problems as well as to anticipate tomorrow's opportunities. Align your observations and recommendations with the strategic goals of management, so that they will resonate with your client.

Moving in the organization's power centers will increase both your visibility and your access to the information you need to provide even better input—ideally, before strategic decisions are made.

Demonstrating the Value of Counseling

"The power of communication departments is frequently informal. . . . Communication departments need power within senior management in order to make strategic contributions. These contributions, in turn, lead to greater power and influence in management decision making,"[9] as Dozier, Grunig, and Grunig point out.

Your contributions won't necessarily be recorded in company documents or acknowledged formally in a meeting. If you aren't sure where you are in the evolution of your role, Howard offers a refreshingly blunt measuring device: "If you are being called in only after decisions are made, you are not practicing PR counseling."

As Howard describes: "Counseling is much more than offering advice. It acts as a strategic glue, bringing together input from all available external and internal sources. Effective counseling selectively sorts information, while focusing only on events that are important and contribute to understanding. A good counselor will relate and interpret the facts; a great one will understand and enhance the meaning."[10]

Developing and expanding client relationships are the manager's responsibilities. On a regular basis, the public relations manager should:

- Listen carefully to identify the client's changing needs and priorities.
- Learn as much as possible about the organization and industry.
- Focus contributions on the organization's strategic goals.
- Demonstrate how these contributions help achieve strategic goals.

1.2: Tips for Agency-Client Relations

No two clients can be handled exactly the same way, but there are general rules that will help you strengthen the manager-client relationship and provide the best possible level of service. Public relations counselor Jean Farinelli suggests following these steps:

Do Your Homework
Immerse yourself in your clients' affairs. Learn their strengths and weaknesses. Get abreast of inside politics that exist.

Do Business Their Way
Learn their business operating methods. Talk the same language.

Develop a Human Rapport
Probe personal interests and ambitions of client personnel. Show them that you're part of their team despite being hundreds of miles away.

Counsel the Client Until You're Blue in the Face
When an opportunity arises to take a position, to contribute your thoughts, take it. Create a client dependency on you.

Never Stop Selling
Develop your own friends among sales people inside the company. Remember, many PR campaigns are sold before you ever make a formal presentation.

Deliver Results and Report on Them
Don't be afraid to spend over budget if you can show results to justify it. However, keep your client informed of cost overruns.

Be Unique
Develop a PR operating style that gets your clients excited to see you when you arrive at their office. Boggle their minds with ideas. Stimulate their thinking. Set yourself and your work apart from their everyday routine.

> ### Don't be Afraid to Tell It Like It Is
> Stand up to clients when you have to. After all, they hired you for your PR expertise.
>
> ### Be Competitive with Yourself
> The highest form of achievement comes when you personally feel that you've done the best possible job.
>
> ### Stay Aware of the World Around You
> Today, we are dealing with a proliferation of communication channels. Think broadly, keep expanding your areas of knowledge.
>
> ### Never Lose Faith in Your Convictions
> They will ultimately pay off for both you and your client.[*]
> _____
> [*]Farinelli, Jean, "Tips for Agency-Client Relations," *Public Relations Tactics*, September 1996.

- Recognize that the relationship, the client, the organization, and the industry are constantly evolving.
- Continually educate senior management on the importance of public relations.

Action Plan

1. For each of your most important clients, list his or her top five business and public relations objectives for the coming year.
2. For each objective, list the *specific* activities you are conducting to help achieve those goals.
3. Evaluate your lists according to the following criteria:
   - the clarity of the objectives
   - how well your activities advance those goals

1.3: Surprise! Clients and
PR Managers Don't Always Agree!

What? Your client doesn't see the wisdom of your every recommendation? He makes decisions that you don't agree with? Shocking! But inevitable.

What do you do when you don't like the decisions of the person who signs your checks—or he doesn't like yours? Here is advice from public relations managers Terrie Williams and Jean Farinelli.

Terrie Williams:

Public relations professionals on the whole are optimistic people. We like to say "yes." Our positive energy fuels our ability to present our clients in the best light possible. However, there is a time to say "no." Creative negativity can be a powerful professional tool. Balanced public relations practitioners learn how to turn down clients and tell hard truths. We learn how to craft our work life carefully, using creative negativity to strengthen our integrity and keep our businesses running smoothly.

These are hard lessons to learn. I know from personal experience. It is a daunting task to turn down a much-needed client when you know the fit isn't right or you sense trouble ahead. It's not easy to call a client and tell him that he treated a journalist rudely or made unfortunate statements in public. But if we can't do these things, we can't truly be balanced professionals.

... Creative negativity is telling the truth but helping the clients to understand that they have options. If you do those two things, you will never be accused of falseness. And you will gain a reputation of reliability—something rarer than people think.

When working with celebrities who live on a constant stream of praise, honest appraisal can be disarmingly refreshing. I have had clients thank me for being the only person to tell them the truth about issues others won't dare bring up. How can people learn or better themselves if they are constantly surrounded by sycophants?

One of the best examples of creative negativity that I experienced was at the start of my career. I had interviewed for a job that I was hopeful of getting. I was disappointed and a bit stunned when I was turned down, but the executive who broke the news to me, Leslie Lillien, took the time to tell me why. That information helped me to strengthen my self-presentation. It helped me to grow in the direction of starting my own business.

Here are some examples of how "creative negativity" can work for you:

Tell clients the truth when they ask. Don't couch statements. Find a way to be tactful but give complete information and then suggest solutions.

If you are faced with potential clients that you can see will be trouble, cut your losses and turn them down. You will save yourself aggravation and a bad reputation. An unsatisfied ex-customer is a severe liability.

Assess the strengths and weaknesses of your staff honestly. Often staff members will be glad to acknowledge their weaknesses. Again, give options. Instead of saying, "I know you're not great with sports and that's why I'm not giving you this account," say, "Your strength is in music so I'm going to keep you doing what you do best." Be positive while making an honest and creative critique.

Assess your own strengths and weaknesses honestly. Delegate tasks to those who are skilled in those areas. Don't put more on your own plate than you can handle.

When the public relations industry as a whole embraces these concepts, we'll no longer be known as "yes people" or "flacks." Rather, we'll be seen as coaches and counselors, professionals who see the truth and apply it with courage and finesse.*

Jean Farinelli:

Picture this: you've spent three months researching and compiling a detailed cost analysis for an overseas PR program. You've taken the preliminary steps to set up procedures for implementing the program, presented it, and then nothing. The client sits in a quagmire of indecision. Now what?

All too often, PR practitioners back off the minute the client says "no" or "we don't like it." Too bad, because this is exactly the point where the real job of PR selling begins.

Second-effort selling is a lost art. In part, it's the art of identifying why the client turned you down. In many cases, there are circumstances beyond your control which determine the fate of your proposal: Did you present your ideas to the client while she had fiscal concerns on her mind, or over the phone on an especially chaotic day? Second-effort selling is also the art of identifying when the time is right to speak again with the client and present your ideas a second time. This time, though, be sure to use terms the client will understand and value.

Today, with the ever-changing workplace and the globalization of business, we must view ourselves in a much broader context, not strictly as public relations specialists, but as people who solve business problems. Seeing ourselves in this light will put us more in tune with what CEOs, senior managers and our clients are thinking. Explain your proposals using business terms like "policy shaping," "market opportunities" and "competitive positioning." Terms like "B-roll" and "media placements" are not a part of the client's language. So don't use them.

Using basic PR terms will not get the client to OK your program. However, by using the appropriate business language to explain what your proposal achieves, you will not only catch your clients' interest and attention, but will also lead them to a better understanding of your ideas and a clearer view of the goals you'd like to achieve.

To be truly effective in the practice of public relations, one has to be willing to put one's job on the line every day. Good counseling is not about saying yes. Good client counseling means telling it like it is. Present your position in a way that builds an inescapable circle of logic that leads to the conclusion you want the client to come to.

If you do, it's more likely your client will seriously consider and adopt your recommendations. Oftentimes, clients will come to you with ideas of their own. Don't immediately say it can't be done. Listen closely, discern what they are trying to achieve, and tell them you'll consider it. If upon further reflection the action really isn't possible, you can get your position across in time.

Convictions pay off, so believe in yours. After all, who can advise the client on how to get messages across better than you, the PR specialist? Your convictions will go a long way in persuading the client to undertake a campaign that your expertise, research and intuition tell you is right for the company. Most importantly, if you don't succeed on the first go-around, don't walk off the field. A well-timed, carefully prepared second effort can make you and your ideas a winner.[†]

---

*Williams, Terrie, "The Fine Art of Saying No," *Public Relations Tactics*, October 1996.

†Farinelli, Jean, "Salesmanship Starts when the Client Says No," *Public Relations Tactics*, September 1996.

- the degree to which your clients understand the contributions you are making
4. At your next client meeting, review the objectives and the activities with your client.

Exercises

No. 1: The Client Relationship Audit

How has your relationship with your client evolved since you first started working for the organization? To find out, conduct a relationship audit. Compile the information below:

- the length of the relationship
- how frequently you are in contact with the client
- the nature of those contacts (face-to-face, telephone, E-mail, etc.)
- key situations that strengthened or weakened the relationship
- the kind of work for which you were hired
- the kind of work you requested
- the current state of the relationship
- the trajectory of the relationship

No. 2: Applying the Consulting Models

Broom and Smith offered five role models of practitioner role behaviors to describe the relationship and expectations between PR consultants and their clients. Which of these models best applies to your current relationship with your most important clients? What are the advantages and disadvantages of this model? Which model would the *client* prefer for the relationship? Which would *you* prefer? Based on the recommendations in the chapter, what steps could you take to move the relationship from the current behavior model to the one that you prefer?

No. 3: Supporting the Bottom Line

Review M.S. Thompson's eight-step process in Box 1.1 for conducting a cost-benefit analysis of public relations activities. Use Thompson's recommendations to determine whether your public relations activities are profitable to your organization. Be sure to spell out your list of assumptions for such variables as alternative programs of action, costs, direct and indirect benefits, and effects.

CHAPTER 2

Personnel

We are shaped by each other. We adjust not to the reality of a
world but to the reality of other thinkers.
—Joseph Chilton Pearce

"For many managers, hiring and keeping good people is the
most difficult and most painful part of the job," says Bill
Cantor, president of The Cantor Concern, Inc., an executive search firm. "It shouldn't be. Like every other skill in business,
this one, too, can be learned."[1]

The First Transition—Yourself

Kathy Phipps' leap from staff employee in a government job to
assistant superintendent for Media and Communications Development for the Virginia Beach, Virginia, Public Schools, included
an adjustment period that led her to develop recommendations for
those taking the step into management.

1. If you are joining the staff of a competitor that embraces a
   philosophy different from what you have adhered to in the
   past, make sure your heart is capable of making the switch.
   After all, where the heart goes so goes the mind.
2. If at all possible, take three to four weeks off between jobs
   and do your homework about your new employer. That way,

you will be ahead of the curve on day one. . . . Read everything about your new company that you can get your hands on. On your first day if you already know names, the projects people are working on, publication schedules, and the hot issues that are going to be attracting media attention, you will be ahead of the curve and in a much more relaxed frame of mind.

3. Your best resource is going to be your staff. Court their support, but don't tolerate sabotage. Accept the fact there is going to be some initial trepidation on the part of your staff. And remind yourself that reserve is usually part of the getting-to-know-you process, not a sign of rejection. Do what you can to relieve any tension in the environment.

4. Concentrate immediately on the issues that are troublesome to your organization. If you're in a leadership position in public relations, effective issues management is going to be right up there on your team's list of priorities. During your homework phase, make sure you get well acquainted with your firm's issues.[2]

Of all of the career transitions the public relations manager makes, the most challenging one may be the move from staff member to manager. The increase in pay, prestige and power is initially exciting, but as soon as the first personnel problem occurs, new managers realize that they are operating in a very different world, with a new set of rules, methods, and goals.

The objective is still to get the job done, but now the manager must work through other people to achieve it. This can be particularly challenging when managing exceptionally creative people.

Team Building—The Hiring Process

While the hiring process begins a time of transition for the prospective employee, it is also a time of transition for the rest of the organization. The manager must take time at this critical juncture to reevaluate the organizational goals and determine what people will fit together best to achieve them. This involves a four-step process to ensure that the manager knows exactly who he or she is seeking, recognizes the right qualities in the candidates, and uses the hiring to ensure that the new member of the team will contribute effectively.

2.1: High-Tech Hiring

Public relations managers spend so much time searching for information on-line these days. Why not find employees there as well?

High-tech hiring is on the rise, as innovative employers use the latest technology to find the right people for their organizations.

Web sites like Monster.com (<www.monster.com>) match résumés with the newspaper's help-wanted section, reaching hundreds of thousands of job seekers. This breadth can be good or bad; sometimes these sites may throw the net too wide and the manager can be inundated with responses.

A better alternative may be to post job opportunities on the organization's *own* Web site. Prospective employees can check out the company's own resources to see if job opportunities are an appropriate fit for their skill sets. Managers can tailor and detail the job specifications as much as they wish. To refine the quality of the applications, managers can post a customized application form that includes only the criteria they care about. On the other hand, if managers want to leave it wide open, they can instruct applicants to send résumés, portfolios, and other materials on-line.

There's still no guarantee that the manager won't have to sift through poorly suited résumés, but the numbers may be more manageable. There is one additional advantage to using the organization's site to recruit—on-line applicants have already proven themselves tech-savvy enough to find and contact the organization through the site.

Step One: Developing the Job Description

When managers prepare to hire, they should be as specific as possible in creating the job description. To do so, the manager must identify and prioritize a concise list of requirements. This is an excellent opportunity to take a fresh look at the entire team to reevaluate the duties of each member.

2.2: Who is Working in PR? A Snapshot of Race and Gender

What is the face of public relations? In some ways it reflects the general public, in others it doesn't come close. Here are the ethnic and gender highlights, according to a 2001 survey by *PR Week*.

Ethnic

The PR industry is still predominantly white (89.4 percent vs. 82.2 percent of the population). Blacks (4.5 percent vs. 12.8 percent), Hispanics (2.8 percent vs. 11.8 percent), and Asians (2.1 percent vs. 4.1 percent) are all underrepresented. The biggest increases in ethnic hiring are being made at the junior level, especially in agencies, which are more inclined to offer multicultural counsel.

Gender

The survey identified a 37 percent disparity between salaries for men ($73,000 on average) and women ($53,000). While critics blame sexual discrimination, *PR Week* points out that:

> ...the major cause of salary disparity is explained by age and experience." The average male in the PR industry is 38, while the average age of a typical woman in PR is much younger, at 33.8. Also, men are more experienced, having worked in PR for 11.1 years (as opposed to 8.2 years for women). In fact, there's a very clear polarization. The largest component of men have been in the industry for more than 20 years (17.5 percent); while an identical 17 percent of women (and again, the largest component of

women in PR) have been in the industry for less than two years. Women in entry level positions in PR now outnumber men by 4:1. . . . Another factor influencing pay discrimination is the choice of sector: men tend to work in the highest-paid sectors (financial services/banking, industrial/manufacturing, hi-tech), while women traditionally have opted for sectors where pay is lower (consumer, food and beverage, travel and tourism, and nonprofits). And men dominate in the best-paid practices (crisis communications, reputation management, investor relations, public affairs) while women—often simply because they're younger—work in disciplines which do not pay as well (internal communications, community relations, media relations).*

Education, Influences, and Demographic Mix
In discussing diversity, Kathleen Larey Lewton, CEO and PRSA 2001 chair, noted that:

> PR professionals begin their work by helping companies, clients, and causes understand the world around them, the audiences they serve or seek to reach. In today's world, those audiences are rarely homogenous, and they are rarely all male or all female, all white, or all well-educated. Yet our profession, and certainly our society, does not adequately reflect the heterogeneous world around us. While we've managed to move beyond the male-dominated world that was PRSA when I joined, we're still far from reflecting the multicultural world around us, the world that we're trying to reach through our PR programs. We need to start at the high school level to encourage students to look at colleges with strong PR education programs, to work with our PRSA chapters and our educator members to build a diverse base of professionals-in-training, and then to aggressively reach out to the broadest possible range of potential members at the professional level.[†]

---

*PR Week Web Site <www/prweekus.com/us/index.htm>.

†Excerpts from interview with Kathleen Larey Lewton reported in *Public Relations Tactics*, January 2001.

It is helpful to have key team members review the description the manager develops. When senior management and line managers are included in developing the job description, differences of opinion may emerge about the rate, scope, and duties of the new position. Resolving such issues before the search begins allows everyone in the process to (1) reach consensus on key issues, (2) create a sharper focus for the search team, (3) minimize time wasted on inappropriate candidates, and (4) keep priorities clear once you begin to compare candidates.

In hiring, notes PR manager Janet Reswick Long, "There is a difference between strategic decision-making and unproductive agonizing." To minimize the latter, she advises building consensus up front on what key traits and competencies a candidate must possess, and determining in advance who the ultimate decision maker is; almost inevitably, you won't have complete agreement among different interviewers.

"Hiring today frequently involves a team of company interviewers across many levels and functions," she explains. "The hiring manager should share the vision of the position with everyone who will meet the candidate. In the survey, nearly 40 percent of respondents complained that interviewers were not prepared or focused."[3]

Bill Cantor points out that the job duties are only one factor you need to consider. He suggests three other considerations:

- the candidate's skills and personality
- the skills and personality of the people to whom he or she will report
- the nature of the organization

Step Two: Screening

Once managers know what kind of employee they want, they can begin getting the word out. Publicizing the position may include placing announcements in professional publications, local newspapers, and on-line job sites; word-of-mouth inquiries to competitors, clients, and contacts in related industries; networking through professional organizations; and the use of professional search services.

The manager should ensure that anyone involved in screening the first wave of résumés is fully aware of the requirements for the position. This information should be presented in written form, including a copy of the position announcement; it may also include a discussion of how the the criteria for the position were developed. Investing the time at the beginning of the process will pay off by keeping the screening process focused. Clear, concise criteria will help to resolve disagreements among members of the evaluation team during the screening process.

When the manager and the screeners have identified key candidates, they need to determine what qualities, tangible or intangible, the team wants to know about each candidate that can't be found on their résumés. Obtaining this information is the goal of the interview, and the better prepared the interview team, the better the hire will be.

"A successful hire starts with good internal communications: a team-driven process in which every interviewer understands the opening as well as what kind of input he or she is expected to give about the candidate," reports Long. "Distinguish who will evaluate technical skills and who will address more general factors like how well a prospect will fit into the office culture. The candidate will benefit from a balanced set of questions and perspectives."[4] It is the manager's responsibility to ensure that this set of interviews gives the organization and the candidate what each is seeking.

Step Three: The Interview

While both the candidate and the organization want to look good in the interview, the manager must make the interview more meaningful for both sides. Neither side is served if significant information is hidden or major issues are not addressed up front.

Long notes that in a boom economy, or seller's market, the manager has to work hard to win over the best candidates. She advises: "Shift your mind-set from buyer to seller. Employ the same approach you use as a PR practitioner to compete daily for media attention. If you're good at media relations, you stand out by presenting clear, compelling information, respecting time lines, and giving

2.3: Personality Traits to Look for in a Hire

Evaluating personalities is an inexact science; managers are never quite sure what makes a candidate tick, and there is no reliable way to test a candidate's on-the-job temperament. Still, Bill Cantor, who specializes in PR executive searches, says successful practitioners need "the ability to persuade without offending." He writes: "It comes down to being likable; practitioners who are cheerful, diplomatic, positive, good listeners and who don't take themselves too seriously are usually very effective in reconciling opposing groups without being coerced or scuttled in the process. Another important point: people tend to support the views of those they like."*

Cantor cites these qualities shared by successful practitioners:

- Response to tension
- Individual initiative
- Curiosity and learning
- Energy, drive, and ambition
- Objective thinking
- Flexible attitude
- Service to others
- Friendliness
- Versatility
- Lack of self-consciousness

*Cantor, Bill, "Winning Personality Traits: Ten Characteristics That Indicate Whether an Individual Will Be Successful in Public Relations," *Public Relations Journal*, June 1983.

2.4: Make the Writing Test Count

A well-crafted writing test measures a lot more than spelling and grammar. When managers use a writing test to evaluate a potential employee, they should consider the advice of Christopher Dobens, vice president of Creamer Dickson in Basfor's Irvine, California, office:

> Every candidate at our agency must take a comprehensive writing test. I've seen a few really good ones, but most are mediocre at best. Perhaps this is because it's far more than just a spelling test. Our test is designed to measure a candidate's ability to write—and think—both clearly and effectively. Basic grammatical competency and an understanding of AP style are merely the fundamentals. We want employees that write clearly and proficiently, and we won't accept anything less.
>
> As painfully dismal as many of the tests are, it is still fascinating to see how a person's thought process is reflected in their writing. From the way they approach the subject matter down to what details they include and omit, the writing reveals much about the way a person thinks.[*]

[*]Dobens, Christopher, "The Lost Art of Writing in Public Relations," *Public Relations Tactics*, April 1999.

thoughtful answers. Treat every candidate you speak with like your media contacts."[5]

The manager should use the interview both to provide and obtain information. She should provide the candidate with a thorough overview of the job, including reporting lines; work assignments; individual, departmental, and organizational goals; and evaluation methods, and time frames. The manager can use the candidate's résumé as a starting point for discussion of work history, education, professional affiliations, career goals, and other related matters. Depending on the position's responsibilities, the manager might want to request writing samples and require that the candidate complete a writing and editing test.

A candidate's interpersonal approach is more important for PR hires than for hires in other industries, because success in the public relations industry depends on good interpersonal communication. Questions about interpersonal and management styles may be answered through the interview process; the manager may still want to ask very specific questions about the candidate's approach to coworkers, clients, and members of the media. The manager might pose a series of scenarios based on current clients and media contacts to ascertain how the candidate would react in each case. Before and after the interview, the manager should observe how the candidate treats other members of the organization—not only upper level managers, but also support staff and other employees.

Once the interview is concluded, the manager should pay special attention to the quality of the candidate's follow-up, since this activity is also essential to the public relations function. Does the candidate establish and follow up on the next step in the process, to ensure the continuation of the relationship? Does the candidate respond promptly to questions and unresolved issues? Overall, is the candidate tactfully encouraging the process and providing the assistance needed to advance the hiring decision? This is the approach managers would want their employees to take with clients and media contacts. A candidate should be taking this same approach with members of *your* organization from the beginning of your relationship.

Step Four: Decision Time

Any unresolved questions should be followed up with a telephone or face-to-face interview before the decision is made. If it is an aptitude issue, retest. If it's a personality issue, the manager should include additional managers in a follow-up interview to get their reactions.

The hiring decision is critical, and the manager should do everything possible to make sure the right decision is made. A mismatch will not serve the organization or the candidate.

Once the decision is made, the manager should sell the hire firmly and positively to all involved—the candidate as well as fellow employees. The organization is about to change, and the success of this transition depends on a positive start.

Outsourcing—A Growing Alternative

One key decision in acquiring help for an organization is whether to hire or outsource.

According to one 1998 study, 73 percent of respondents who work in corporate PR departments or agencies said their organizations outsourced activities. The most frequently outsourced activities were writing and communications (73 percent); media relations (45 percent); publicity (38 percent); strategy, counseling, and planning (37 percent); and event planning (32 percent). Speech writing, research, community relations, crisis communications, and graphic arts/publication design were also identified.

The decision to outsource usually comes straight from the top, reported the survey by Bisbee and Co., Inc. and Leone Marketing Research, both of Orlando, Florida. Public relations vice presidents, department directors, and account supervisors were most likely to decide if a public relations activity would be outsourced.[6]

Outsourcing is on the rise for three reasons:

1. It can be cost-effective.
2. New technologies allow more versatile outsourcing arrangements.
3. It allows for significant flexibility—a particularly important advantage when the workload in an organization fluctuates.

"Initiatives by whatever name—reengineering, restructuring, reinventing, downsizing—often go hand in hand with major increases in outsourcing," reports Carole M. Howard, former vice president-public relations for the Reader's Digest Association, Inc. She says that "many corporations have a very simple guideline: If it can be done cheaper outside while still maintaining internal quality standards, send it out."[7]

Jennifer Bisbee, president of Bisbee and Co., Inc., has this advice for managers who are thinking about outsourcing:

> On the client side, be sure to outsource for the right reasons—outsourcing is a decision that can have a long-term impact both on your public relations department and on your entire organization. Understand your business' corporate culture.... Understand which departmental functions are essential to your organization's core business. Some functions, such as crisis management or customer relations, may be better handled internally; others, such as newsletter production, may be conducted more efficiently by a vendor.
>
> Look at outsourcing over the short- and long-term. Short-term projects, like a special event, are ideally suited for a vendor to implement. Others, such as a proactive publicity program, will require a more long-term approach. A vendor can lay the groundwork, but ask yourself this question: Can your organization devote the manpower to sustain the activity?
>
> Consider the ramifications of outsourcing. If you plan to outsource for the long term, be clear of the potential opportunity costs. What impact will outsourcing have on the professional development of staff members? Will outsourcing affect how your target audiences view the organization?
>
> Set clear, realistic goals. Whether you want to save money, increase productivity, become more flexible, or improve your organization's ability to react to opportunities faster, it's important to explicitly lay out your goals before making an outsourcing decision. Achieving those goals will help you sell senior management on more outsourcing in the future. To prevent problems, decide what you want from a partnership ahead of time, and clearly state those expectations to the vendor. Include these in the contract; specify daily, weekly, or monthly reporting times; and create benchmarks for evaluation to keep the relationship

on track. Goal evaluation also helps you determine if the vendor is a good fit.

Choose your vendor carefully. There are several ways to improve your chances for a good client-vendor fit. Ask peers whose opinions you value to refer you to trusted vendors. What is the nature of your outsourcing and what expertise does the vendor need to bring to the table? Check the vendor's references. Spend time interviewing the vendor. Ask for and review samples that are akin to the project at hand. And listen to your intuition.

Stay involved and accessible. If your goal is to completely walk away from a PR function once you have outsourced it, think again. You will need to manage the vendor's work, coordinate it with internal functions, and keep senior management apprised of your department's progress. Also, stay accessible to vendors; a good one will be motivated and self-reliant, but will still need ongoing input from you to help achieve the goals you have set forth.

Teamwork is the foundation of a successful outsourcing relationship. The more mutual sincerity, honesty, and respect you have with your vendor, the more successful your combined efforts will be.[8]

Keeping Employees

Hiring is an expensive, lengthy, unsettling process for an organization. Once the hire is made, managers should protect their investments in hiring by fostering loyalty and productivity as much as possible. The manager who helps employees improve and enhance their skills provides them with the opportunity to grow along with the organization.

Creating a Corporate Culture

Managers in the public relations business have recently begun to look more closely at the corporate culture in their own organizations.

The common complaints of many workers—long hours, poor internal communication, stressful conditions—are particularly pervasive in the public relations business, according to David Paine, president of the California communications company Paine & Associates. He notes that:

> To the credit of many agencies and dedicated leaders in the field, efforts are being made to run agencies with greater vision from a "human resource" perspective. However, agency life remains famous for its lack of effective operational leadership and management. Today, it's still about the billable hour and not too much more. . . .
>
> Until agencies and other companies change the way they view their most important "asset," until they start seeing their employees as "people who just happen to be working, instead of workers who just happen to be people," they'll never receive the kind of discretionary effort that comes from the heart. They'll never get the energy, creativity, loyalty or enthusiasm that makes good agencies great agencies. . . .
>
> Employees are human beings and as such, they have certain inner needs that have to be met in order for them to be happy and motivated:
>
> - They need to be honestly informed at all times, about everything.
> - They need to have a say in what happens to them and their job.
> - They need to be treated fairly and equally.
> - They need to be accorded common decency and respect.
> - They need to contribute, feel good about what they are doing, and be appreciated.
> - They need to work in an environment that is free of competition with peers.
> - They need to have balance in their lives and have the opportunity to grow personally as well as professionally.
>
> Whatever values a company eventually adopts, these fundamental principles should be expressed somewhere within them.[9]

Paine also stresses the importance of organization at the management level:

> Nothing undermines a well-meaning organization more than poor management and lack of process. The best of intentions on a values level will quickly be buried under by inefficiency, waste, conflict and everything else that goes with a poorly run organization.
>
> Agency leaders need to work real hard to identify the processes they need to be effective, then continually improve them in ways to allow the company to run well, and provide high-quality service to clients, and a great work environment to employees.[10]

Immediately after an employee begins work, the PR manager should formally introduce the new member of the team to the organizational philosophy. If the organization has a written values statement (and it should), make sure the new employee has a copy of it. If there is no written version, the PR manager should at least inform the employee verbally about the values and practices that guide the organization. Set aside time to review the specifics of the statement and explain how the organization's philosophy applies to specific work situations. An employee who is exposed to the philosophy early and formally will learn the organizational perspective faster. An employee who is exposed to the philosophy in action—the PR manager acting according to the code—will have the philosophy reinforced on a regular basis.

While the organization's values statement is the guiding set of principles, the manager should also encourage employees to personalize their approach. If it is too "top down" without room for individual input, the philosophy becomes onerous and dictatorial—it stifles rather than channels creativity. The PR manager should be particularly cautious about this danger with public relations employees, since they are frequently more creative and free-spirited than those in other industries, and may be more likely to initially reject any formal code. Ultimately, the manager must demonstrate to the employee that the company code is liberating rather than binding.

Job Ownership—Accountability and Empowerment

Employees work harder and better when they know what their goals are, how to do their jobs, and how they will be measured. The PR manager can help in all three of these areas.

Communicate to your employees as clearly as possible what you want them to achieve—this helps create focus for both of you. Make the objectives as clear and measurable as possible. Whenever possible, include input from the employees in setting the objectives, for two reasons: (1) the employee may know more than you do about the client or project, so the goals that are formulated may be more useful, and (2) the employee will normally work harder to achieve goals that he or she has helped to develop.

How much guidance does an employee need? Obviously, this will vary from person to person, but the PR manager should work to ensure that all employees feel comfortable approaching the manager to discuss strategies and ask for feedback. Employees who feel confident in their jobs, or comfortable in consulting their boss to find solutions they don't have will be more productive and positive about their work environment.

When the manager provides clear, measurable objectives, the employee can self-monitor throughout the project to determine how things are going. At the conclusion of the project, the employee and manager can review the original objective, how effective the work was, and how the process can be improved the next time around. Employees who feel responsible for the final product will be more diligent during the process and will gain more satisfaction when the project is complete.

Employee Training: The Basics and Beyond

Writing skills remain the most useful tool of the public relations business and managers should constantly reinforce the key concepts of

2.5: Cultivating a Culture in a Virtual World

Establishing a workplace culture with your employees is hard enough in a traditional setting. It is even more challenging as more organizations meet only in the "virtual office."

"In the absence of a widely understood and adopted corporate self image, the rise of telecommuting threatens to erode the sense of belonging, achievement and purpose that for centuries have been primary workplace motivators," says Sharon VanSickle of Portland, Oregon's KVO Advertising and Public Relations. "Corporate culture is not something you plant. It is something you grow. Influencing corporate culture takes finesse and patience."*

VanSickle suggests four steps to building a lasting corporate culture.

1. *Research*—thoroughly understanding employee's perceptions of the company.
2. *Looking Within*—examining internal and external communications to see how the company described itself and its work force.
3. *Defining Yourself*—developing a definition of your corporate self, a definition that should be:
   - Specific
   - Measurable
   - Appealing
   - Consistently executed
4. *Implementing*

As the number of virtual offices increases, managers must bring the workforce together on a regular basis and use face-to-face meetings as a chance to create meaningful interpersonal interaction among members of the team.

---

*VanSickle, Sharon, "The Importance of Workplace Culture in the Age of the Virtual Office," *Public Relations Tactics*, December 1996.

effective writing to all employees. Suzanne Sparks FitzGerald, author of *The Manager's Guide to Business Writing*, emphasizes these concepts:

- Know your readers.
- Feature the "you attitude" and stress benefits for the readers.
- Know your single communication objective or purpose.
- Be clear, economical and straightforward.
- Use subject lines, indentation, short opening paragraphs, and postscripts.
- Write strong introductions and conclusions—the reader may read only the beginning and the ending.
- Use headings, white space, and visuals to prevent reader strain.
- Write actively (subject-verb-object) rather than passively.
- Avoid negative writing.
- Use the power of persuasion to influence readers.[11]

While writing is central to the public relations profession, it is not the only responsibility of the professional. The manager should also assist members of the department in developing skills in research, media relations and basic business skills. Workshops and seminars on these topics can introduce key concepts and provide background. The manager can help employees apply newly learned skills by delegating tasks related to workshop topics. Managers who develop management skills in other employees are then free to do alternative work that can benefit their organizations. Along with reinforcing the basics of the business, the manager can offer professional and financial incentives to encourage employees to take advantage of professional development opportunities. This helps develop more productive, valuable employees, and increases their loyalty.

Professional organizations such as the Public Relations Society of America (PRSA) offer conferences, seminars, and even distance learning courses to help public relations professionals develop or improve management and professional skills. Some of these seminars are industry-specific.

Employees who are committed to professional development may want to earn accreditation in the industry. PRSA's Accreditation Program is designed to unify and advance the profession by identify-

---

2.6: Creating a More Inclusive Work Environment for Gay Men and Lesbians

Box 2.2 examines the workforce according to two demographic variables: gender and race. The PR manager should also be aware of another variable in the personnel mix: sexual orientation. The increasingly diverse public relations workforce necessitates an increased level of awareness and understanding on the part of managers. Mark Abelsson, director of workplace education for the Gay and Lesbian Alliance Against Defamation (GLAAD), suggests a number of ways managers can ensure a fair and inclusive work environment for all employees:

1. Adopt, promote, and enforce nondiscrimination policies which encompass sexual orientation.
2. Extend to gay and lesbian employees the same benefits enjoyed by heterosexual employees, including medical benefits, bereavement leave, and parental leave.
3. Train all employees on sexual orientation issues in the workplace.
4. Support lesbian and gay employee affinity groups the same as other groups.
5. Use inclusive language in all personal and company communication.*

---

*Abelsson, Mark, "Creating a More Inclusive Work Environment for Gay Men and Lesbians," *Public Relations Tactics,* March 1999.

ing those who have demonstrated broad knowledge, experience, and professional judgment in the field. The program is open to members of partner organizations who have at least five years of paid, full-time experience in the field.[12] For more information on fees, applications, study guides, and other materials, contact:

> The Universal Accreditation Department
> PRSA Headquarters
> 33 Irving Place
> New York, NY 10003-2376
> (212) 460-1436 or (212) 460-1464

Find Fun in the Job

Of course, a big part of your job is focused on the bottom line. But remember, the best public relations employees are usually intellectually curious people who enjoy challenge and stimulation. Make sure your environment reflects that approach.

Mix things up once in a while. Do something employees wouldn't expect out of management. Despite the pressures of the job, lighten up and do something that reminds your staff that you are a person of intellect and improvisation, and that you appreciate these same qualities in them.

Reward your employees in unorthodox ways, taking them to unusual places or providing them with unusual perks. Get everyone out of the office once in a while. Your organization is designed to communicate creatively to achieve an objective—take the same approach in your communications to the people who work with you.

Action Plan

Whether you are a one-person shop, the manager of a large internal PR department, or the director of a large agency, it is important to evaluate current and potential staffing needs on a regular basis.

1. List each of your clients and their *specific* current public relations needs. This list should include the services you provide as well as the services provided by others.
2. Project the needs of those clients for the next year. Consider all possibilities that would affect their needs: new product introductions, personnel changes, movement into new markets, new manufacturing processes.
3. Repeat the process for prospects you would like to win as clients within the next year.
4. List all the services you currently provide. Be honest and specific. Go beyond "writing services" and "media relations" to identify core and auxiliary services. If you manage a group of people, consider organizing the list according to the skills and services provided by each person in your organization.
5. Compare the lists to identify the strengths and weaknesses of the personnel in your organization, guide you in developing employees to strengthen and diversify your services, and assist you in developing job descriptions for new hires.

Exercises

No. 1: Where Do You Want To Go Today?

You may have an adequate understanding of the contributions of your employees, but do you know where they want to be in a year? Do *they* know? A career planning session with each person who reports to you can be beneficial. Let them know the purpose of the meeting, and give them a set of points you would like to discuss. Include as points for discussion their current performance as well as their aspirations and future contributions to your organization. This sends a strong message that you are investing in their development while encouraging them to focus on it as well. The meeting shouldn't be part of the annual review process, because that is so closely tied to raises and bonuses. Instead, it should focus on how the employee can grow to provide additional contributions to the organization—a win-win situation.

No. 2: Vendors and Clients—
All Part of the Chain

Your suppliers can do a better job if they know where you are going. You can do a better job for your clients if you know where *they* are going.

As part of your interaction with vendors and clients, urge them to think about—and communicate—their plans for the future. Maybe your vendor has other services to offer—listen and determine whether they would work for you. Perhaps your client is considering moving in a radical new direction—one that could have a significant impact, positive or negative, on the services you provide. The earlier you know about the potential change, the better you can staff and plan for it. Exchange lists with each of your vendors. On the list you give your vendor, write additional products and services you are considering developing in the near future. On the vendor's list for you, ask him to list any additional products or services he might be able to provide to help you do your job. Long-term planning needn't be part of every discussion, but be sure to include it on a regular basis so that you're not surprised by anyone in the chain.

No. 3: Exploring the Outsource Option

Is work in your organization completed as efficiently as possible? Consider both quality and cost, and consider outsourcing. Many managers turn to this option only to fill a temporary staffing gap. But outsourcing can be explored at any time, and a good manager should constantly reevaluate the work process to ensure that goals are achieved efficiently. Outsourcing can provide additional flexibility and allow you to use vendors with superior skills in a specific area.

Again, a list method can be useful. Write down the major projects and activities your organization accomplishes, then list the resources and costs associated with each one. Be thorough to account for all costs. Consider your outsourcing options for each project. Can a specific vendor do this work cheaper or more efficiently and deliver the same quality? Look for opportunities to reduce costs and improve your services by outsourcing tasks to vendors who might be less expensive, better qualified, or both.

CHAPTER 3

Research

Can you think of anything more permanently elating than to
know that you are on the right road at last?
—Vernon Howard

I
n many boardrooms, management and public relations may
appear to be diametrically opposed. According to this view,
management is a highly organized, upper-level function that
emphasizes planning and analysis to determine how to allocate
resources most efficiently to achieve objectives. Public relations, on
the other hand, is viewed as almost a clerical function, used to
send out information after key decisions have already been made.

How can the PR manager correct this misconception? Through
research. Meticulous, relevant research is one of the most important,
tangible ways that PR managers can legitimize their function and
make significant contributions to an organization.

"Without research, practitioners are limited to asserting that
they know the situation and can recommend a solution," state Cutlip,
Center, and Broom.

> With research and analysis, they can present and advocate
> proposals supported by evidence and theory. In this context,
> research is the systematic gathering of information to
> describe and understand situations and to check out
> assumptions about publics and public relations conse-
> quences. It is the scientific alternative to tenacity, authority

and intuition. Its main purpose is to reduce uncertainty in decision making.[1]

Most managers expect—and respect—research. They require their staffs to regularly answer specific questions: Where are we now? Where are we going? How are we getting there? Are we doing this as efficiently as possible? Public relations, on the other hand, appears to have a more ambiguous function. Therefore, PR managers must work even harder than their peers to conduct thoughtful, practical research that answers these questions.

Think like the boss. Clients are looking for demonstrated results, and research can help them get it. Good research produces findings that help develop policy and measure results, which are in line with your client's or organization's strategic objectives. Research provides a deeper, more comprehensive understanding of markets, customers, and competitors; guides management in allocating resources; and, best of all, makes the ambiguous concrete. When you use research properly, you are functioning as management. In fact, "participation in management increases when practitioners do research,"[2] Cutlip, Center, and Broom report.

Research Reduces Uncertainty

PR managers who use research effectively can impact the highest levels of their client's organizations because they help management achieve the ultimate objective: reducing uncertainty in decision-making. Research will be most useful if managers understand the organizations' strategic objectives, extract key findings from existing relevant information, employ the most direct means to collect additional data, and synthesize their findings in forms that are comprehensive, focused, and easily understood.

This chapter examines the key tools used in public relations research and discusses the best ways to present research findings to management.

The Research Template:
Problem Statement and Situation Analysis

Regardless of the client or objective, research begins with the problem statement and situation analysis.

The Problem Statement

The problem statement clearly identifies the goals of the public relations campaign. The statement should be as concise and direct as possible: written like the lead of a news story, it should present the five basic news elements (who, what, when, where, and why) in order of importance. The statement should be formulated in collaboration with senior management. This will help ensure that management is focused on the program from the outset and that the statement and resulting public relations work reflect the organization's key strategic goals.

The problem statement is critical: the more clear, concise, and connected to management objectives it is, the greater the chance of success for the subsequent research and campaign.

The following are examples of useful problem statements:

1. Next calendar year the Brendan Bottling Company will introduce a one-calorie version of its soda, Binkie. During the year, the company wants 100 percent of the distributors of one-calorie Binkie to understand that the primary selling points of the new soda are the sweeter taste and the reduced calories. The company wants 80 percent of the current consumers of Binkie to understand these selling points and 50 percent of the current customers to try the one-calorie Binkie at least once during the year.

2. DJL Soccer is announcing the recall of its Powerfoot! soccer balls. In the next six months, DJL will reach 100 percent of the consumers who purchased Powerfoot! soccer balls in the past year and inform them of the recall.

The clarity of these problem statements will help keep the public relations activity focused and simultaneously provide a quantifiable goal that can be measured at the conclusion of the program.

The Situation Analysis

The situation analysis is the collection of all information relevant to the problem statement. It lists everything managers need to know to conduct their public relations. The situation analysis draws together all existing research findings (secondary data) which, in turn, will help to identify where information gaps exist and where managers need to conduct their own research (primary data).

The situation analysis also helps to establish a baseline, or benchmark, for future measurement of the effectiveness of the public relations activity. By clearly identifying the current situation, the manager ensures that there will be a point to measure against in the future.

Methods: How to Find
What You Need

Once the managers have focused on the problem, learning what they know and need to know, the next step is to find the information that's still lacking. It's time to conduct primary research.

In the physical sciences, research conjures up images of test tubes and petri dishes, but in public relations the subject is human behavior. The manager employs the social sciences, an approach that can be described as "systematic listening." The social sciences are no less scientific; they simply use different methods.

Remember that the question drives the method—don't let the tail wag the dog. Managers must first figure out what they need to know, then figure out how to get that information. A manager who starts out by saying, "We need a survey" is making a mistake. The first statement should be, "We need to find out how many people recognize and like our product." Only then can the manager determine what method—survey, focus group, participant observation, etc.—is most efficient at finding the information that is needed.

In most situations, there is usually a significant body of information that has already been collected—secondary research. This can include sales reports, market analyses, quarterly and annual reports, census data, industry studies, and any other relevant information. Managers who review this information can (1) increase their understanding of the organization's position and history; (2) triangulate data—bring together information from various sources to increase their understanding of "the big picture"; and (3) help identify misconceptions or knowledge gaps that need to be addressed.

Once the managers have examined the existing formal data, they can go "straight to the horse's mouth" to learn more. Managers shouldn't assume that they have to go outside of the company to get started—key resources are usually inside the organization, and there's a good chance that no one has ever asked their opinion. Excellent sources may include: product managers, salespeople, company veterans who understand the organization, clients, and other members of the industry. Identify and establish relationships with the most thoughtful, professional people in the organization, and ask for their input. Explain how their participation in the research process will both help the organization and help them, by presenting their ideas to management. These people can provide immediate insight as well as connections to other valuable resources.

When managers have drawn what they can from within the organization, they conduct focus groups of key constituents outside the organization to gather more information. The focus group brings together people who represent the views of clients, vendors, and/or community members. Focus groups allow exploration of the attitudes and perceptions of the group in-depth. Some findings can be developed only through such a dynamic group process.

A focus group should include between a half dozen and fifteen people—large enough to stimulate conversation, but not so large as to become unmanageable. It can be conducted at the offices of the

3.1: Web Essentials

If you need information fast, consider the following Web sites as described by PR manager Dennis John Gaschen, APR. Keep in mind, however, that the fluid nature of the web has a downside: this list is subject to change at any time.

Research

If you can't afford Lexis-Nexis <www.lexis-nexis.com>, the on-line newspaper research service, try the following research portals:

- <www.bartleby.com> has a full-text searchable database of reference, verse, and classic literature that contains more than 200,000 Web pages, including more than 22,000 quotations and 4,765 poems.
- <www.refdesk.com> links to a large collection of directories, publications, almanacs, and encyclopedias.
- <www.gallup.com>, the site of the Gallup Organization, one of the world's largest management consulting firms, offers a searchable archive of past polls.
- <www.zoomerang.com> allows visitors to create surveys and gather and analyze the feedback. Surveys can be E-mailed to a client list, posted on the Web, or sent to a zoomerang database for a fee.

Search Engines

- <www.dogpile.com> sifts the top search engines and combines the results.
- <www.google.com> has a clutter-free design that makes for quicker load times.

Aggregators

- <www.about.com> consists of more than seven hundred Guide sites neatly organized into 36 channels. Visit "About Public Relations" for articles, directories, forums, and a free newsletter.

- <www.online-pr.com> provides links to media, references, and PR resources.
- <www.pr-education.org> is a comprehensive aggregator of PR-related sites and services.
- <www.prplace.com> lists Internet addresses and hot links to PR organizations and publications, on-line news services, and databases, and journalism interest groups, as well as lots of how-to information on the PR field.

Business Tools

- <www.ceo-express.com> provides links to a wide array of handpicked on-line resources. From breaking news, investment information, and company research to travel tips, sports scores and continuing education resources, the site features more than 40 categories of targeted, concise information.
- <www.lionshares.com> provides stock ownership information and analysis. Simply enter a symbol in the search bar to find the top institutional, mutual fund, and insider owners of any public company.
- <www.sidcato.com> is a site for the best and worst annual reports. It's a must for anyone who's involved in what many consider to be a company's most important document.

E-mail

- <www.theultimates.com/email> has a common interface to the six different E-mail directories on the Internet.

Grammar Guides

- <www.jargonfreeweb.com> is a Web site maintained by the Gable Group and its exclusive Jargonator, which rates the jargon content of your next release on a 1 to 6 scale.

Marketing

- <www.mediapost.com> is targeted to media buyers, PR professionals will benefit from its array of audience numbers and statistics.

- <www.personalization.com> is a fantastic resource for how to market on-line. It focuses on what makes on-line marketing and PR different from the rest of the business world.

News

- <www.poynter.org> provides journalists with reliable information, useful tools, and provocative suggestions. PR pros can benefit from its specialized search engine that collects stories daily from journalism sites (about four hundred newspapers, broadcast outlets, and on-line sites) around the Web and around the world.
- <www.individual.com> provides free, individually customized news, information, and services to business people over the Internet. News and information are organized in a way that lets you quickly and efficiently read what you need to know each day.

News Groups

- <groups.google.com> allows high-speed access to newsgroup postings already archived.

Trends

- <www.e911.com> is maintained by the Lukaszewski Group and focuses on crisis communications planning, strategic crisis response, and litigation visibility management.
- <www.frost.com> is dedicated to strategic market information, analysis and trends for a score of different industries.

World Wide Web

- <www.mediametrix.com> monitors on-line service usage and then posts the most visited sites. Check out its Top 50, Global Top 50, and Top 500 lists.*

---

*Excerpted from Gaschen, Dennis John, "Web Sites You Need to Know About," *Public Relations Tactics*, May 2001.

organization if you are not trying to hide the sponsor. Managers can conduct focus groups themselves or bring in professional facilitators. If the managers choose to lead the group, they must keep the objective of the process clear: they are there to collect information—to listen, observe and learn—not to convince anyone of their position or to sell the company. The more neutral the focus group facilitator is in phrasing questions and responding to answers, the more likely the group is to yield useful data.

The focus group not only helps collect critical information from key publics, it also helps improve relations between the public relations manager, the organization, and the participants.

If the organization requires a broad response to specific questions, the manager should consider conducting a survey. Because the goals of survey research are more specific than those of other forms of research, the manager must decide at the outset exactly what audience the organization needs to reach, what questions the audience should answer, and what form will be most useful for the responses. Surveys can be conducted by telephone, through the mail, or in person. Public relations managers can design and distribute the survey themselves, and tabulate and interpret the findings on their own, or they can employ a professional polling organization for each step.

Finally, the PR manager should take advantage of electronic sources for research, as detailed in chapter 6. Databases can be useful for trend research and big-picture issues; Web sites of organizations and associations can provide useful data about industries; and chatrooms and E-mail traffic can be used to track real-time responses to changing situations.

Delivery: Packaging Your Findings Effectively

Once managers have collected all relevant information, they need to synthesize the data to ensure that management receives the most important information, supported by quantitative and qualitative analysis, in the most direct and persuasive form.

At this stage, the manager should resist the temptation to include every detail of research methods and instead focus on what others need to know. What are the key objectives of management? What questions stem from these objectives? Which findings most thoroughly and directly answer those questions?

3.2: Evaluating Clipping Services

As communication goes electronic, so goes monitoring. PR veteran Kelly Schmitt, vice president of Luce On-line, Inc. offers this advice on evaluating the new, electronic clipping services:

> Begin by finding out what kind of monitoring the service offers. Do they monitor everything in print that can be delivered electronically? Does the service also clip from the Internet/on-line news publications? This is an important question, because what appears in print is not necessarily what appears in the publication's Internet/on-line edition. And don't forget the countless e-zines and broadcast sites that do not have an off-line equivalent.

> You'll need to ask exactly what it is they're searching. Any bona fide clipping service can provide you a list of their news sources for both their electronic clipping and Internet/on-line clipping. You would never buy a new car without knowing which options are included. Use the same judgment when choosing a clipping service.

> One of the most important questions to ask is how your service is conducting its searches. Are they using a search engine? Are humans gathering items through manual searches or are they clipping from the actual source? You must also ask if they're simply reaching the publication's index page, or if they monitor all sections of the paper/site. These searching variables will significantly impact the type of coverage you receive.

If you're satisfied with their answers, you need to inquire about delivery methods and times. If you need to be the first to know, then you must select a provider that can deliver in real time. Real time is defined as 24-hours, seven days a week. If you can afford to wait, then you'll want to know if delivery is daily or weekly, and at what time of the day. Find out in what format the clips will be delivered. This can include full-text clips, abstracts, or summaries. Delivery can be to a personal news Web site, to the service provider's news site, or an alert method that tells you that you have news that you need to retrieve. You'll also want to inquire as to whether on-line and print clips are delivered together or separately. This will be important if you want to identify the news source.

Each provider structures its pricing differently. Some offer contracts that carry a service fee and a charge per clipping. Others charge by the term, but do not have any clipping fee. It is imperative that you know what the contract terms are—they can be from one month to one year. Also, be sure to inquire about any setup fees or cancellation charges.

In this era of virtual employees, you'll want to make sure your clipping service offers solid customer service. Who can you talk to if there is a problem? What if you need to change or add search terms? What if you're going to be out of town and need to send all the information to a colleague? Make sure your electronic clipping service has a customer service department that is friendly and willing to help out. Don't be afraid to ask if you can talk to your future customer relations representative before signing on.

Electronic clipping services are designed to take the hassle out of media monitoring. You shouldn't be typing, searching and deciphering on your own. By asking the right questions of your future electronic clipping service from the start, you can be relatively at ease when you make your final choice.*

*Excerpted from Schmitt, Kelly, "Don't Get Clipped by Clipping Services," *Public Relations Tactics*, May 2001.

Some senior managers think in big-picture terms and prefer only the broadest findings and recommendations. At the other end of the spectrum are managers who enjoy delving into the numbers— either to verify interpretations or to explore the data for other useful findings. It is best to match the presentation to the style of the reader, but managers rarely all think the same way. The PR manager can achieve some middle ground in reports by providing an executive summary and overview at the beginning, followed by more detailed analyses and ending with appendices of raw data. This allows broad thinkers easy access to key findings while providing background as desired for more detail-oriented managers.

Even the simplest software programs now allow managers to produce a variety of charts, graphs, and infographics in reports. These are helpful as long as they clarify data, but don't go overboard on the visuals. Remember that management prefers a straightforward data analysis that provides the clearest possible picture of each topic and leads to logical, understandable recommendations.

Action Plan

Write a research plan for each client:

1. Write a clear, concise problem statement.
2. Conduct a situation analysis. Gather as much information as possible to develop a thorough understanding of your client, your client's objectives, the context for the public relations, and any other factors that may affect the program.
3. Once you have assembled this information, identify the gaps. Determine what information you need that you don't have.
4. Conduct primary research to fill the gaps.
5. Assemble all secondary and primary information in a form that is easily comprehended and referenced by management. You are now ready to develop recommendations for your plan.

Exercises

No. 1: Demographic or Psychographic—Which Works Best?

For audience analysis, identify which market characteristics are most important to research. Your client may be tempted to tell you, "We need to know as much as we can about every characteristic of our audience," but that won't help. Prioritize. What matters most—demographic (race, gender, age, income) or psychographic (attitudes about the product, self-perception) information? By figuring out what you *need* to know, you are more likely to find it.

No. 2: Basic Benchmarks

Determining benchmarks should be an objective of any research. When you evaluate your program later, you will need to compare your findings with your starting point. Benchmarks also help focus a public relations program so that everyone agrees on what you are trying to achieve. Develop benchmarks for each client and each program.

No. 3: On-line Audit

Web sites provide background and immediacy. Develop a list of sites that you can refer to on a regular basis to keep you and your clients up-to-date on critical issues. Visit each site regularly, even if briefly, and alert your clients to the most important breaking stories that can affect their business.

CHAPTER 4

Crisis Communication

If economics is the dismal science, then
contingency planning is the abysmal science.
No one likes to look into the abyss.
—Disaster recovery consultant Kenneth Myers

At all times, it is better to have a method.
—Mark Caine

Airplane crashes. Financial difficulties. Executive scandals. Product tampering.

Each day public relations managers see crises in the news and say, "Whew, I'm glad that's not *my* company." But the manager's job is not to wish away potential difficulties, it's to help avoid them and manage them when they do occur.

Even the most carefully run organizations are forced to deal with crises, because many situations that can damage an organization are beyond its control. This chapter explains how public relations managers can identify the most likely crises, organize and train a crisis communications team, and develop and implement a plan that will minimize the harm to relationships with key publics when a crisis occurs.

Identify Potential Crises

The time to begin managing a crisis is before it happens.

The first step is to identify and prioritize potential crises. Begin by looking at the company history and inviting employees throughout the organization to provide input. "The plan will be more successful if employees have some ownership of it,"[1] note Guth and Marsh.

Ask specific questions: What problems have occurred before? How frequently? Have the conditions that contributed to earlier crises changed?

Next, look industry-wide. Consult with professional groups and trade associations in your business to understand what types of crises have occurred and to identify industry-wide trends that might herald potential crises. When it comes to crisis communication, don't reinvent the wheel. Take advantage of the lessons learned by others by reviewing the crisis history of your industry. Contact industry associations to determine what crises have occurred most frequently in the past. Identify competitors who have handled crises well, as well as those who have handled crises poorly. Compare the communications plans of each to identify how you can improve your own plan. Interview key planners from organizations who have experienced crises to see what went well, what went poorly, and what they would do differently.

Finally, look at crises that transcend the industry. Some crises, such as unusual stock price fluctuations or employee misconduct, can occur in any industry. Develop a thorough list of potential crises, and prioritize them according to potential impact and probability.

While public relations managers are primarily responsible for communications, their responsibility as managers in the organization extends further. "The goal of risk assessment is not just the identification of potential hazards," Guth and Marsh point out. "Once each threat is identified, steps should be taken to eliminate or lessen it."[2]

They add, "many organizations can avert crises by clearly articulating and actively implementing their core values. By doing so, they can make all aware of the legal and ethical limits under which they choose to operate."[3]

The Crisis Plan

The crisis plan includes selecting and managing a crisis team, developing a written plan, and training personnel throughout your organization.

The Crisis Team

The PR manager should decide who will be part of the crisis team, selecting participants based on the skills needed, the departments that will require input and, of course, the ability to operate under pressure. An early strategic decision is the determination to have one team for all crises or specialized teams based on the nature of the crisis.

Don't limit the scope to the communications function; the team will also need input from the legal department, operations, safety, finance, and top management. If the business deals with exceptionally complicated products, include a technical representative.

Some fellow managers may not see the benefits of membership on this team. If they need persuading, the PR manager should remind them that crisis planning provides two advantages to participants: (1) an opportunity for each to take a fresh look at corporate policy and possibly make changes, and (2) the chance to rectify situations that could lead to crises.

The crisis team functions as a high-speed microcosm of the parent organization. The PR manager is responsible for clearly defining each member's roles and responsibilities. Establish a clear chain of command and a flowchart to ensure that information will be collected and disseminated and decisions made on a timely basis during the crisis. What information will be needed, who will collect it, and how will they communicate it to team members?

This flowchart should be agreed to by all key members, yet have enough flexibility to meet the changing demands of a crisis. Clarify the division of labor by developing concise checklists for each participant. Prepare a backup plan for both people and processes. Remember, an emergency might exclude crisis team members from the process.

Establish a representative speaker for the company. This is a critical decision that must be made before the crisis occurs. Designating the chief executive officer (CEO) will increase credibility but also means that you won't have your spokesperson's full attention; the CEO has more than communications to deal with during a crisis. A PR official acting as the spokesperson should improve communication between the organization and key publics, since this official will already have strong relationships in place; however, this decision may antagonize groups who want information directly from the company's top official. Depending on the severity and length of the crisis, as well as the communication skills of the CEO, the PR manager may choose to have the CEO make the first and most important statements while PR personnel are used for interim communications. The PR manager should also identify a second public speaker to step in if for some reason the first is unavailable. Finalize these decisions in the planning stage.

The Plan

Your written plan should include only the essentials. If it's too long or too detailed, it will be difficult to keep up-to-date and no one will use it. Make it concise and flexible. Essentials include:

- Name and contact information for team members
- Work checklists for each team member
- Name and contact list for key audiences (including the media)
- Contact list of local government organizations (fire, ambulance, EPA, inspectors, township/city officials)

Be sure that lists cover as many contingencies as possible, including after-hour contacts.

Public relations managers should treat the written plan like a living, breathing entity—a guide that is as dynamic as the environment in which your organization operates. Regularly update all information. Treat a crisis for a competitor or a business in a related industry as an opportunity to assess how your own plan might work in similar circumstances. If no crises occur, continue to review the plan with members of the team on an annual basis. Whenever a significant change occurs in your organization, be sure it is reflected in the crisis plan.

Training

"The first key to putting out your fire is to act like real firefighters and train like crazy. Prevention begins with media training, for your staff

4.2: Drill Dynamics

An important tenet of crisis management is to continually test the crisis plan. Here are some tips from Richard K. Long, professor of communications at Brigham Young University, on how to make your test effective:

A tabletop exercise involves small groups that work on a scenario for two to three hours, clarify roles, and propose solutions. Then, as in all drills, a postmortem would identify what went well and not-so-well.

A larger version would become multifunctional, including human resources, legal, safety, environmental affairs, and others.

A full-scale drill, as commonly practiced in many industries, engages internal teams and external resources such as police and fire departments, hospitals, and outside counsel. Some companies include local reporters who usually play their normal role as the askers of questions. Occasionally, though, it's educational to ask a reporter to serve as company spokesperson.

A few cautions are in order.

First, be sure the scenario is realistic and plausible. Some senior executive will ask why you're spending time (and money) on a situation that "couldn't happen to us."

Second, scenarios should provide for "developments" caused by demands for information from reporters, elected officials, investors, and others. This pace of change can paralyze organizations, particularly if PR practitioners become focused solely on the news media.

Third, when planning a full-scale drill on a company site or school campus, alert your neighbors. With the recent cases of workplace violence and school shootings, it's quite possible to scare neighbors who don't realize the SWAT teams, ambulances and fire trucks are only part of a practice session.[*]

---

[*]Excerpted from Long, Richard K., "Realistic Drills Enhance Survival in Crisis," *Public Relations Tactics*, January 2001.

and your client," says Kathleen Hessert, president of the Charlotte, North Carolina-based Sports Media Challenge.

> The Red Cross has done all kinds of studies that prove that you will slow down your absorption of information at least 100 percent in trauma. So if you're in the middle of a crisis and you're trying to train somebody how to deal with the media, how to understand what your strategy is, how to make sure they've got the tactics to do it you are really fighting uphill.[4]

The training program should include not only the members of the crisis team, but, to a lesser degree, all employees in your organization. During a crisis, members of the press and other publics may contact anyone in the organization, so employees who are not designated spokespeople should be directed to minimize their comments and direct all inquiries to the spokesperson. At the same time, all employees should be instructed on how they can obtain information during a crisis.

Training for upper-level managers and team members will depend on resources. At a minimum the public relations manager should provide management and team members with an opportunity for input to the plan, a written copy of the final plan, and an overview session that explains everyone's role in the process. In-depth training may involve tabletop exercises, media training, and even full-scale rehearsals involving simulated crises.

Anatomy of a Crisis

Guth and Marsh's Crisis Dynamics Model divides the evolution of a crisis into four stages:

- *The Warning Stage*, when the PR manager can be proactive and at least partially control events before they happen.
- *The Point of No Return*, when the crisis becomes unavoidable, some damage will occur, key publics become aware of

the crisis, and the PR manager is forced into a reactive mode.
- *The Cleanup Phase*, when the PR manager must deal immediately with the crisis and its aftermath.
- *The Final Stage*, when things return to normal, although by definition the crisis has, in some fundamental ways, changed the definition of "normal" indefinitely.[5]

When a crisis begins, urges public relations counselor Rene Henry:

> . . . put the public interest ahead of the organization's interest. Your first responsibility is to the safety and well-being of the

---

4.3: Know the Nets: Intra and Inter

In a crisis, speed is essential, so you need to use your intranet and internet tools as effectively as possible.

Intranet

An organization's intranet ". . . gives communicators another tool to use as they try to manage employee concerns, rampant rumors and intense media focus,˚ " writes Curt Anderson, president of the Birmingham, Michigan-based Corporate Web Services. Anderson cites Ford Motor Company, U.S. West, and General Motors as companies that have used their Intranet systems to reach employees and other key audiences during crises.

At the same time, Anderson cautions that

> Intranets are a passive communications tool. Employees must seek or "pull" information from it. Because of this, an Intranet won't always be the best place to turn when a crisis erupts. When the infamous tapes were released that revealed Texaco managers complained about diversity programs, they faced a blizzard of public criticism. While the company's extensive external PR efforts are well documented, the employee com-

---

munication challenge was just as daunting. The company's nascent Intranet didn't seem to be the appropriate tool to speak to employees about the corrective action being taken. Instead, the company used the tried-and-true "push" E-mail and satellite broadcast technology to get important messages to employees.

Internet

Diane Witmer, author of *Spinning the Web: A Handbook for Public Relations on the Internet*, cites Swissair and Procter & Gamble as companies that have used the Internet effectively in crisis situations.

When a Swissair flight crashed into the Atlantic Ocean in September 1998, the airline "immediately implemented its crisis communication plan, which involved extensive use of the internet," said Witmer. "Because Zurich-based Swissair is an international carrier and flight SR111 involved three countries (the U.S.A. departure, Canadian accident site, and the Swiss destination), the internet was an excellent vehicle to reach appropriate target publics."[†]

Procter & Gamble uses the Internet to deal with a variety of rumors about the corporation and its products. Witmer uses the example of a rumor about Febreze, a P&G product designed to remove odors from fabrics. When a rumor began circulating on the internet that the product was unsafe for use around pets, P&G "... acted quickly, and created an area of the Febreze Web site that is devoted to 'Pet Safety.'" Witmer says, "The Web page conforms to good public relations practice by not repeating the rumor verbatim, but by referring to it and then providing information from credible sources to refute it."[**]

Intranet and Internet communications should always be part of the overall strategic approach to communications—but when time is of the essence, they may be tools that you go to first.

---

[*]Anderson, Curt, "Using an Intranet During a Crisis," *Public Relations Tactics*, May 1997.

[†]Witmer, Diane F., *Spinning the Web: A Handbook for Public Relations on the Internet* (New York: Addison Wesley Longman, 2000), 181.

[**]Ibid., 183.

people involved. Once safety has been restored, face the public and face the facts. Never try to minimize a serious problem or "smooth it over" in the hopes that no one will notice.[6]

Collecting and distributing verified information will be paramount, particularly when the crisis erupts, since both the media and interested publics will want to know what is happening, and if they can't find out from the organization, they will go elsewhere. Bad news delivered honestly or directly will hurt your organization less in the long run than stonewalling, report public relations researchers Allen Center and Patrick Jackson.

> People tend to get reassurance concerning their physical well-being and safety largely from believable information that pierces through the uncertainty, the rumors and the gossip. Human nature, fortunately, has a toughness about it, enabling most people to handle substantial bad news or physical danger by making adjustments.[7]

When a crisis breaks, Henry recommends this strategy:

- Bring the situation under control, if possible. Always protect people first and property second.
- Analyze the situation to judge its newsworthiness. Don't create a crisis by jumping the gun. Many times the situation doesn't warrant media attention.
- Gather the facts—who, what, where, when, why, how, what next.
- If necessary, activate your crisis management team. Act quickly; spare no expense to distribute the information you determine the media and others should have.
- Give the media as much information as possible; they'll get the information (perhaps inaccurately) from other sources.
- Don't speculate. If you don't know the facts say so and promise to get back to the media as soon as possible. Then be sure to do so.

4.4: What You Shouldn't Say in a Crisis—and How You Shouldn't Say It

Your spokesperson should be forthright in dealing with media questions during a crisis. There are, however, some questions he or she simply cannot and should not answer. Rene Henry advises organizations in crisis to avoid direct comment on:

- money estimates of damage
- insurance coverage
- speculation as to the cause of the incident
- allocation of blame
- anything "off the record"

Your spokesperson should never respond to media questions with "no comment." This answer can imply a lack of cooperation, an attempt to hide something, or a lack of concern. There are more appropriate responses. Some examples:

"We've just learned about the situation and are trying to get more complete information now."

"All our efforts are directed at bringing the situation under control, so I'm not going to speculate on the cause of the incident."

"I'm not the authority on that subject. Let me have our Mr. Jones call you right back."

"We're preparing a statement on that now. Can I fax it to you in about two hours?"*

---

*Henry, Rene A., *You'd Better Have a Hose If You Want to Put Out the Fire* (Windsor, CA: Gollywobbler Productions, 2000).

- Protect the integrity and reputation of the organization.
- Report your own bad news. Don't allow another source to inform the media first.
- Perform an act of goodwill during or immediately after a crisis when appropriate and possible.[8]

4.5: Handling High-Profile Cases: PR Lessons from Athletes in Scandals

Considering the specialized world of sports public relations? Consider some of the crises that occur, and solutions that can be implemented, from author Ty Wenger:

Dennis Rodman kicks a photographer in the groin. Michael Irvin is accused of assisting a rape. Albert Belle pelts a photographer with a baseball. Oksana Baiul is arrested for underage DUI.

OK—you're their sports publicist. What do you do?

The first question to ask yourself is whether a crisis really exists. In today's world of outrageous sports personalities, multi-hued hairdos, cross-dressing heroes, and braggadocio-as-marketing, a PR agent's "crisis" could be a marketing agent's "campaign." You should make your first step in a crisis to the marketing or advertising department to find out how they plan to portray your athlete or your sports entity.

However, if you've checked with your marketing department and determined that your client's latest foray into marital infidelities or casual assault is not part of their game plan, it's time to shift into damage control.

Poor training isn't the only obstacle you and your client can place in your path. Hessert adds that you're fighting an even greater uphill battle if your athlete hasn't already created a reservoir of goodwill, even more so if your client has crafted a notorious reputation.

Ultimately though, despite all your best efforts at prevention and training, . . . your relationships with your media contacts, and how effectively you use them, will mean the difference between resolving your crisis and letting it burn out of control. As Meredith Geisler, director of public relations for Fila USA, says, it pays to have friends in high places. "With a friend in the media, oftentimes you can bounce some ideas or bounce a fax off them, so they can help you better prepare for the onslaught of the media attention," Geisler said. "But oftentimes you also have to offer this friend an exclusive or the first dibs at whatever the story could be. Because there are probably few things that are more infuriating in the media than to be barraged with good news and soft news from publicists and, when the crisis hits, the publicist or athlete is totally inaccessible."

As Hessert says, if you don't retain the power of your media relationships and thereby the control of the information, you're about as useless as a one-legged field goal kicker. "If they don't come to you first to get that information, and believe what they get from you, then they're going to go to other sources," she says. "And if those other sources are more credible or are more apt to give them the information at the time, then you lose a great deal of the power that you would have had otherwise."

And if that happens, you and your wayward jock may have nothing left to do but apologize. As hard as it may seem to imagine Dennis Rodman or Michael Irvin offering a heartfelt mea culpa, Geisler says falling on the sword can always be your option of last resource: "It's amazing how often a simple apology works. If the client or the athlete says, 'you know, I'm sorry, I erred, and I feel horrible about it,' oftentimes that goes a long way."*

---

*Excerpted from Wenger, Ty, "When the Sport Hits the Fan: Crisis PR in the Age of Athlete Scandals," *Public Relations Tactics*, March 1997.

Aftermath

Crises end at different rates for different audiences. When the press stops calling, it doesn't mean that everyone has lost interest in the situation. Once the crisis is under control, PR managers should use their communications to "officially" end the crisis mentality and assist the media in moving on to the next phase. This can be done by changing the tone and language of the communications to reflect resolution and movement into the next phase. Work through media contacts and use controlled, non-mediated forms of communication (direct mail, newsletters, public forums, etc.) to reach key audiences. Keep all interested parties up-to-date on the organization's efforts to rectify the situation and to reduce the chance that it will reoccur.

Continue to monitor press and public reactions to the crisis and aftermath as closely as possible, and be prepared to respond to any additional inquiries or misinformation. Don't assume that things have returned to normal. The organization's credibility may be at a low point after a crisis, and the PR manager may have to increase communication efforts to restore relationships. Use this increased communication—with members of the media as well as other audiences—to evaluate your crisis communications plan.

Once PR managers are reasonably sure that their relationships with key audiences have been restored, they should formally debrief the crisis team and upper management. Even under the best of circumstances, it is rare that everything goes exactly as expected. This is the time to review and improve your plan before another crisis occurs.

Finally, remember that a crisis plan is really an extension of the overall strategic public relations plan. Establishing and maintaining relationships with key publics is a long-term objective, and the strength of these relationships will be integral to success during a crisis.

Action Plan

1. Identify the most likely and most potentially damaging crises that could impact your organization.

2. Develop a list of key personnel and contact information to be used in the event of a crisis. Include internal as well as external personnel, along with emergency numbers for key support groups such as government agencies. Submit the working list to everyone who might need it before you finalize and distribute it.
3. Put together a crisis team and delegate responsibilities in case of an emergency. Schedule the team to meet at least annually to update crisis response systems.
4. If possible, test your team by conducting a mock emergency.
5. If an emergency occurs, conduct a debriefing when it has passed to evaluate the team response and improve systems for future crises.
6. A good crisis communication plan is an offshoot of a good public relations plan—keep in contact with all key audiences on a regular basis in order to maintain the benefits of an established relationship when a crisis occurs.

Exercises

No. 1: Perfecting the Company Spokesperson

Identify who will speak for your organization in the crisis. Consult with management on this decision, and spend time helping the speaker prepare. This can include everything from staging mock press conferences to developing policies on what information will be distributed and what will not.

No. 2: The Missing Link

What happens if key people are unavailable during a crisis? If your organization suffers from a fire, earthquake, or other emergency that makes key personnel unavailable, who will take over their responsibilities? Train managers for different roles and ensure that there is an agreed-upon chain of command in case someone is unavailable.

CHAPTER 5

Finance

Wealth is the product of man's capacity to think.
—Ayn Rand

If the world could be divided into left-brainers and right-brainers, it would be safe to toss most public relations practitioners into the right-brain bin. Most are, by nature and training, "word people" with a creative, nonlinear bent, and because they spend so much time dealing with words, few ever get comfortable with numbers.

If practitioners want to progress to management, they have to change that, but the change is not as hard as many practitioners fear. A thorough review of the basics will help ground the practitioner in this critical part of the business.

This chapter introduces you to three important aspects of finance: internal budgeting, financial relations with clients, and financial public relations.

Budgeting

Before they become managers, practitioners focus on getting their jobs done. After they become managers, they focus on getting the job done—within budget.

Practitioners may know how to write a release, organize a press conference, and report activities to a client, but do they know how to determine what each activity *costs*? And how do you assemble these costs into a comprehensive budget?

Good budgeting benefits both the agency and the client. It is also critical for public relations managers to develop systems ensuring that they are fairly compensated for the services they provide. This practice generates profits and enhances a manager's reputation. Those who work at cut-rate prices will be perceived as providing cut-rate service. Managers must understand their costs and value and implement a consistent approach to calculating both so that they can produce budgets that are fair *and* profitable.

Begin by developing a list of services provided. For each service, write down everything done for a client—and that means *everything*.

Each service can be expressed in terms of expenses, grouped into standardized costs:

- *Salaries and Benefits*: These can be calculated as a function of time; that is, the percentage of your employees' time devoted to a project or client. Be sure to include administrative time as well as costs for part-time employees and consultants.
- *Production*: These include costs for photography, printed materials, artwork and design work. Most agencies include a markup on these expenses to cover their administrative costs and financing costs prior to reimbursement.
- *Overhead Costs*: This can be calculated either as a percentage of time or actual cost for items such as rent, postage, and utilities. Don't forget salaries and benefits for support staff.
- *Travel/Entertainment Expenses*: These are reimbursements for expenses related to client meetings, travel and entertainment for media relations, etc. These costs normally do not include a markup.
- *Additional Costs*: Some projects develop or expand unexpectedly and some crises require immediate and extensive services. Keep track of all time and material expenses for each project, particularly those that include unexpected activity.

The budget for a client or project consists of the accumulation of all services, grouped according to these standardized costs. Budgets can be developed on a monthly, quarterly, or annual basis, based on the client's reporting requirements and the agency's reporting system.

The better that managers understand the standardized costs of each kind of PR service, the more confidence they will develop in budgeting. The budget process also serves as a useful, constant reminder of the connection between time and expenses. By emphasizing time management in the organization, managers can offer clients top-notch service and still turn a profit, and by comparing cost estimates with actual expenditures as a project progresses, they can monitor the accuracy of the budget and adjust as needed.

Financial Relations with Clients

Chapter 1 included a brief discussion of finance as it relates to client relations. This section deals with the preliminary discussions with potential clients and standard contracts for public relations services.

Depending on the client's preconceptions, the initial discussions about fees and payment schedules can be complicated. Clients who have never purchased public relations services are frequently suspicious. They may have heard negative comments about PR people, they may not understand how public relations works, and they are wary of a service that cannot guarantee results. Managers should acknowledge and address these concerns as needed, so that discussions are based on a full understanding of the contract's service and terms. A full and frank discussion up front will minimize later misunderstandings about the goals and costs of public relations.

There are three basic contract forms: retainer, project-basis, and contingency.

Many public relations organizations prefer a **retainer** contract, in which the client pays a regular, ongoing fee to an agency for an agreed-upon level of work, usually expressed as a number of hours per week or month applied to a particular set of goals. The terms of the retainer contract vary from client to client, but most are paid on a monthly basis.

The retainer plan offers advantages to client and agency. The first is stability. The client can project costs and the practitioner can project revenues for a set period. More important, though, is the arrangement's longer-term commitment. A retainer contract reflects a client's understanding that an effective public relations program takes time and that the practitioner will have to spend resources on research, media contacts, and other groundwork before the manager can provide the client with tangible public relations benefits, such as story placements.

An alternative to the retainer is the **project-basis** arrangement, in which manager and client agree to a set fee for the development and implementation of a particular project. Some clients opt for this arrangement initially so they can evaluate the agency's efforts before committing to a longer contract. This arrangement is also well suited to special events, one-time projects or product rollouts. While clients like the fixed cost and clear results of this arrangement, it comes at a cost: Single-project public relations is rarely effective because it is contrary to proven communication theory. Effective communications requires a systematic, long-term approach. One-shot projects are less useful for developing the relationships with key audience members and media contacts that can be the real strength of a public relations program.

A third approach is the **contingency** contract, in which a fee is paid based on a particular outcome. As will be discussed in chapter 8, many professionals frown on contingency contracts for several reasons—mainly because of their risky nature. Some public relations objectives (such as coverage in a particular media outlet) simply cannot be guaranteed.

In developing their contracts and setting fees PR managers should be sure to educate the client about the philosophy behind the arrangement.

The Contract Review

At some point during the client/agency relationship, the client will usually ask for a review of the contract. This may be done on a scheduled basis, may result from the manager's failure to meet client expectations, or could be necessitated by a change in personnel or policies on either side.

The contract review is stressful for the manager. The agency's work is being evaluated and the contract may be in jeopardy, but a review can also be helpful to both sides. It provides a fresh look at the public relations environment and, if handled well, may actually strengthen the manager's case with the client. The review's outcome may hinge on its real purpose: whether it is intended as a simple update to adjust programming and budgets, or to provide the client a wholesale evaluation of the services. Some reviews are based on the concept of zero-based budgeting. Here the manager is asked to justify the goals, methods, and costs of each program in the plan. The philosophy is to start with a clean slate and include only the elements that are considered the most essential.

Regardless of the contract structure or frequency of review, managers should assume that the client's premise will be, "What have you done for me lately?" In other words, managers are only as good as their last games. With frequent changes in management and business plans, clients demand quality service on an ongoing basis, regardless of their history with the agency.

Financial Public Relations

The communications needs of every organization vary, but there is one area where everyone needs to communicate: money. Nonprofits and for-profits, small businesses and large, all need to communicate with key audiences about finances. This is a high-profile area of public relations, because top management keeps a sharp eye on the bottom line in any organization.

Investor relations are a critical segment of this type of public relations. Companies rise and fall on the faith of current and potential investors. "Much of the effort of the investor relations program is directed toward enhancing the credibility of the corporation inside the financial community," writes PR expert Jerry A. Hendrix.

> The financial media, security analysts, shareowners, and potential shareowners must have a favorable image of the corporation ... Prospective shareowners, financial media people, security analysts and others targeted for communication are invited to as many corporate functions as possible. The ultimate form of 'audience participation,' of course, is the actual purchase of shares in the company.[1]

The tools of the trade for financial public relations include projects that target current and potential shareholders (annual,

---

5.1: Reporting Financial Information

Reporting financial information doesn't have to include convoluted phrases or jargon, notes Christian Anderson, public relations manager for Footaction USA:

Case in point: Quarterly earnings news releases. An earnings release, where the primary audience is made up of analysts and financial editors, is not the place to show off your feature-writing skills. But that doesn't excuse the hundreds of earnings releases issued every three months that are so poorly written that they leave the reader confused and exhausted. Fifty-word sentences, three-inch-long paragraphs, randomly and/or incorrectly capitalized words, a complete disregard for AP style.

The problem, says Anderson:

Many of these releases are being prepared by folks outside public relations or corporate communications, such as finance or legal. Frequently, they're more concerned with meeting SEC requirements and obscuring disappointing results than what

---

semiannual, and quarterly financial reports, Web sites, shareholders' meetings); government-related projects (financial filings, legislative efforts); and projects directed toward the financial press and analysts (press releases, conference calls, corporate presentations to analysts, corporate summaries, Web sites, direct mail campaigns, media monitoring).

A key difference between financial public relations and other kinds of public relations is the degree of government oversight of the communications. Publicly traded companies must communicate financial information according to the regulations of the U.S. Securities and Exchange Commission (SEC), an environment that affects the content, form, and distribution of this information.

The original goal of these SEC regulations was to ensure that information distributed by publicly traded organizations was accurate. In recent years, however, the SEC has added regulations to ensure

their writing looks like. Others originate from investor relations people grounded in finance. Unfortunately, however, many have been prepared by PR people who either can't write or whose solid writing disappears under a barrage of edits from the CEO or general counsel.

Anderson's advice:

- Use bullet points to help readers find important financial data.
- Break up large chunks of copy into smaller, more manageable ones.
- Shorten long sentences by using active verbs and eliminating needless words.
- Review the AP and New York Times stylebooks to get a feel for language usage and rules for spelling, capitalization, abbreviation, and punctuation.
- Lay off the fancy words and jargon-filled phrases.*

*Excerpted from Anderson, Christian, "Financial PR: Opportunities by the Numbers," *Public Relations Tactics*, July 1999.

that a variety of publics understands the financial information that all information affecting current and potential investors is released in a fair and uniform manner to avoid selective disclosure.

The SEC is not alone in its concern. In the last two decades, consumers have grown increasingly intolerant of indecipherable and incomplete disclosures—and highly suspicious of companies that appear to release information selectively or unfairly. The percentage of Americans who invest in the stock market has increased dramatically during this time, and these new investors want to be sure that they have the same access to information as professionals and long-term investors.

Pressure from government and investor organizations increased dramatically in the early 2000s, when companies such as Waste Management, Enron Corporation, and WorldCom—as well as accounting firms such as Arthur Andersen—were involved in very public crises over accounting practices and financial reporting. This pressure will continue to increase through the decade, while media and public monitoring of financial public relations will also increase.

This combination of factors makes it essential for the manager to appreciate the new environment for financial public relations. To minimize problems with the SEC and maximize credibility with relevant publics, the goal of financial public relations should be to release all financial information in the most direct, easily understandable form at the same time to all audiences.

Summary

The financial area of public relations is one of the most important—and neglected—parts of the business. By familiarizing themselves with the concepts and methods used in this area, public relations practitioners can take a significant step toward management.

Budgeting allows the manager to track developing public relations programs and provide timely, useful reports to management. Familiarity with basic contracts helps the manager to develop a relationship with clients that is based on clear, honest communication.

And finally, a solid grounding in government regulation and accounting principles allows the manager to contribute to an organization's financial public relations, a function that is closely monitored by the highest-level managers in any organization.

Action Plan

This action plan aims to familiarize you with your clients' financial situation as well as more generic budget and finance issues.

1. Review your clients' annual reports, including footnotes, to gain a full understanding of the report and the company's performance over a number of years.
2. If you work for a publicly traded company, review your company's annual report. Learn how you and your department fit into the company's overall structure, and examine the company's performance over time.
3. Review the annual reports of competitors for your company and your clients, to see how they are doing in comparison to similar organizations.
4. Think budgets. Ask to see your department's budget and see where you fit into it. Develop specific strategies to help the department meet its budget and share them with your supervisor.

Exercises
No. 1: Build Your Own Budget

You may know your company's financial plan, but what is your personal financial plan in the organization? Develop your own budget for work, assigning hours, and costs to each project that you are assigned. Work with your supervisor to see if your individual budget is in line with his estimates for each project, and adjust accordingly. This will make you more sensitive to money—and time as well.

No. 2: Issue Your Own Financial Report

Top management focuses on long-term performance; you should, too. Summarize the budgets you make, so that you can present management with an annual financial report related to your work. List projects accomplished and break down time allocated to different tasks. Make the report—and your contributions—clear and concise.

No. 3: Contribute to the Company's Annual Report

For years, investors have complained that annual reports are dull, confusing, and poorly organized. The reports reflect the input from key levels in the organization—legal, financial, etc.—but these contributors are not necessarily thinking in terms of communication. You are, so who better than *you* to improve the reporting of financial data? Volunteer to help with the writing portions of the report, offering drafts of letters from the president and summaries of the business climate. This can showcase your skills, provide contact with key members of management, and, in the end, help improve your organization's most important form of communication.

CHAPTER 6

Technology

Every contrivance of man, every tool, every instrument,
every utensil, every article designed for use, of each and
every kind, evolved from very simple beginnings ...
—Robert Collier

The greatest challenge and opportunity in public relations management today is in the area of technology. Managers face a dizzying array of communications technologics that influence every area of the profession, from research to developing business proposals to the final evaluation of campaigns.

And yet, while media technologies change daily, innovations are adopted at different rates: a few professionals leap at any opportunity to explore cutting edge technology; others cling to arcane pre-computer systems; most are somewhere in between. Public relations managers must ensure that they are working with the most useful technologies and that they are familiar with those used by their clients and key audiences.

Most of the new technology has made *gathering* information easier, but *controlling its flow* more difficult. With the increase in the means of distributing information (fax, E-mail, Web sites, etc.), managers have been forced to address new systems designed to *screen out* too much input, such as iMiva screening and Send mail.

Managers have also redefined the idea of "timely" delivery of information. The network evening news gave way to CNN's 24-hour presentation, which then gave way to what Steven R. Thomsen calls a "hyperspeed process" that pushes the practitioner to stay ahead of other news consumers by conducting "pro-search."

"Most on-line services, even those that update the databases every 24-hours, still only archive what *has* happened," Thomsen reports. "The new focus of issues tracking and issues management for these practitioners is to 'capture' the 'news' before it may actually be published in mainstream daily or trade press."[1]

Technology has also increased the storage capacity for information, resulting in a knowledge base that now doubles every seven years—and may double every 35 days by 2010. That growth demands that public relations managers rely on ever-more-advanced technologies to collect, organize, and prioritize information.

A Framework for Understanding New Technologies

Regardless of its wonders and promises, technology remains a tool in providing three primary functions:

1. gathering information
2. packaging information
3. disseminating information

This chapter is divided into these same three functions and is designed to help public relations managers evaluate and implement new technologies in creative, cost-efficient, and effective ways.

Gathering Information

Managers now use Internet resources and databases to collect and store information about prospects, clients, audiences, competitors, and industries. Both allow managers to collect more information, in

6.1: WANs, LANs, and Stand-Alones: A Primer on Computer Configurations

You've got to start somewhere with technology, and one good place is the plan for setting up your computers.

Consider work functions and employee interactivity. Analyze not only the current staffing, projects, and workflow, but also your probable needs two to four years out. Then, consider the three basic configuration options: stand-alone computers, local-area networks (LANs), and wide-area networks (WANs).

For a group of individuals working on separate projects, a series of stand-alone computers may be sufficient. Stand-alones are the least expensive way to go but may make future system mergers difficult. Remember that while IBM and IBM-compatible computers dominate in American businesses, most graphic artists prefer Apple systems.

The next step up is the local-area network, or LAN. In a LAN, computers in close proximity are connected with cable or Ethernet to share files. For example, the account manager can access a copywriter's draft on one terminal while a graphic designer checks it out on another. A LAN means committing to specific hardware and software.

The next step up is a wide-area network, or WAN. A WAN consists of a series of linked LANs, mainframes, or both, connected through a system that is carried by a telephone carrier or cable company. Graduating to a WAN brings new management concerns, foremost among them the distribution of processing power and system security. Complex systems allocate computing power according to need. They may, for example, centralize all of the processing power in one large unit. If the system allows contact with vendors, customers, or anyone else outside the company, managers should assume they are linked with the Internet and must thoroughly research and address data access and system integrity.

more detail, faster and cheaper than ever before, producing finely honed and near-instantaneous analyses that would be impossible with traditional methods. To cite just one example by Petrison and Wang:

> Through creative applications of databases, for example, an examination of customers' demographics, lifestyles, buying behaviors, credit history, and media exposure could lead to a more sophisticated understanding of the consumer's buying process.[2]

Internal Databases

Internal (self-supporting) databases offer privacy, control over data, vast storage capacity, and matchless ability to distribute relevant data throughout the organization. Petrison and Wang describe how a manager might set up an internal database:

> One section of the database may include information on media such as reporter and publication names, addresses, types of computers owned, whether review copies of products are requested, types of products (business or entertainment) covered, a subjective estimate of the reviewer's importance to the company and an estimate of how frequently products are covered. The database system may also be used to keep track of other data, such as product information, review copies and news releases mailed, media coverage received and competitor information.[3]

Managers considering developing an internal database should ask:

- What information can a database provide that I am not getting?
- How much time and money will a database *require*, compared to systems already in place?
- How much time and money will a database *save*, compared to systems already in place?

- Who will create the database (in-house or outsourced personnel)?
- Who will maintain it (in-house or outsourced personnel)?
- Who will have access to which information?

External Databases

External (on-line) databases offer many of the advantages of in-house databases, along with greater scope and unique early-detection and monitoring capabilities that alert the manager to the latest changes in finance, a particular industry, or other area of interest. But the on-line systems also have disadvantages:

- Limited ability to control and package information
- Varying quality and timeliness of information
- Overwhelming amount of irrelevant information

Managers considering on-line databases should ask:

- What *specific* goals (monitoring media, prospecting for new clients, examining trends, etc.) would the database help to achieve?
- What current systems could the database replace?
- How quickly do I need the information?
- In what form do I want the information?
- How wide (or narrow) do I want the information search to be?

A customized, on-line database news service can help managers provide optimal service to clients. Consider which qualities are most important to you: breadth of coverage, speed of transmission, or organization of the information. Then select a system. Here are some options and their advantages:

- DataTimes provides access to 200 major U.S. daily newspapers, with updates every 24-hours.
- NewsEdge provides access to more than 100 wire services, newspapers, and broadcast organizations. The service can be customized to automatically download to your computer.
- WordPerfect's Mainstream employs customized profiles of user interests to scan news outlets for appropriate stories, then E-mails them within seconds of the time they are placed on the wire—and hours before they appear in print.

Internet Searches

Managers should fully understand the limitations of current methods used to search the Internet. Different search engines yield very different results and, at this time, none can capture all available information on any subject. Using multiple search engines or meta-engines can help.

Managers who conduct research over the Internet should consider these questions:

- What information, *as specifically as possible*, am I trying to find?
- How comprehensive and relevant are the search engines I am using?
- How comprehensive, current, and credible are the sites that I am accessing?

How does a manager pick a search engine? Witmer outlines the five general types:

1. *Searchable Indices*: Also known as "meta-search" engines, these are massive databases cataloging the contents of Web pages. They generally yield the largest pool of results, for better and for worse. If you use a searchable index, you'll be sure to get as much information as you need, but you also have a good chance of getting more than you can handle.

Examples of searchable indices are Lycos, Excite, and AltaVista.

2. *Subject Catalogs*: A little less comprehensive than the searchable indexes, but still broad enough to bring you large collections of data. These engines provide sets of links presented according to a specific hierarchy, based on your search criteria. Examples of subject catalogs are Yahoo! and LookSmart.

3. *Annotated Directories*: Lists of hotlinks to Web sites on a particular topic, along with brief (one-paragraph) summaries of each site so that you can browse quickly before selecting a site. Examples include Magellan and Lycos Top 5 percent.

4. *Subject Guides*: Subjective annotations for links on a particular topic, of varying quality depending on the appropriateness of the topic and the capabilities of the specialist developing the list. An example of a subject guide is the *W3C Virtual Library*.

5. *Specialized Directories*: The most targeted form of search device, the specialized directory is a compilation of E-mail addresses, newsgroups, postings and Web site addresses, all related to a particular topic. Examples include DejaNews, Four11, and Switchboard.[4]

And, as Witmer points out: "Remember that the tool you choose is based on your research objective. Generally, the more focused your search and the more limited the amount of data you want, the further down this list of search engines you should go to begin your search."[5]

Chatrooms and On-line Focus Groups

Chatrooms allow public relations managers to monitor, and participate in, free-flowing discussions that could be related to a client or product. But these conversations can be disorganized and unmanageable, resulting in few useful results.

A better bet for managers is the on-line focus group. Managers can contact a range of participants through the Internet or more traditional systems and establish a time and place on-line to conduct the group. This method quickly and inexpensively allows people spread over a geographic area to participate in a real-time discussion. These groups may also produce data that might not show up in a face-to-face group, where inhibitions and social constraints can influence answers.

Packaging Information

Desktop publishing, Web site design software, and other innovations continue to offer new opportunities for packaging information.

Desktop publishing systems give public relations managers control over design and production of their materials. From concept through the final product, everything can be done in-house. This can reduce costs, turnaround time, and errors. The development of desktop publishing technology and the capacity to download materials directly from the Internet have greatly expanded the capabilities of desktop publishing. CD-ROM catalogs and Web sites offer a wealth of photographs, clip art, and fonts, making desktop publishing nearly as versatile as traditional printing methods.

Nevertheless, purchasing or upgrading a desktop publishing system carries risks. A manager must commit to a system, code data, customized software, and so forth. Managers thinking of implementing or expanding desktop systems should consider the following:

- What *specific* end products will I be creating?
- What production requirements (color ranges, fonts, typefaces, photographic needs, paper weights, shapes, and sizes) will the system have to handle?
- Will I gain any advantages—in terms of time, cost, and flexibility?
- What is my primary production goal? Am I trying to improve quality, speed turnaround time, or reduce costs?

Each system will also carry staffing implications. Managers should ask:

- Do I currently have anyone on staff who can do this work?
- If not, how long will training take and what will it cost?
- Will I have to hire new talent?

Web Sites

The rush to get on-line and the explosion of technology in the 1990s led to unrealistic expectations about the advantages of the Internet. Many organizations developed sites with little thought to how they tied in to an overall strategic plan. While some sites have been successful, many failed to achieve anticipated objectives—if these objectives were ever identified at all.

The hard-learned lesson: high-tech public relations is really an extension of traditional public relations approaches. An on-line presence is neither the panacea promised in the early 1990s, nor the useless expenditure with intangible results described in the late 1990s—it is a tool that is as effective as the people and strategies behind it.

"[A Web site] positions you ahead of the competition. A professional and interactive look levels the playing field between small independents and large agencies. It allows your expertise to shine and gives you an unfiltered platform from which to broadcast your PR philosophy, articles you have authored, publications and more,"[6] writes Edward J. Barks, president of Barks Communication.

While the business potential of Web sites is undeniable, building and maintaining a comprehensive, dynamic site requires a significant ongoing commitment of time, cost, and talent. Internet users expect a site to be up-to-date, easy to use, and accurate. If it isn't, they won't be back.

Possible negative factors to consider include the following:

- Security is an ever-growing concern, since a site can open your company's doors to hackers.

- A site requires a new level of technological expertise for the organization.
- Universal access to posting information has reduced the quality and credibility of all sites.
- The Internet user group is appropriate for some clients and useless to others. The Internet user profile is evolving rapidly, but it remains a relatively limited audience.

On the other hand, the advantages are equally important:

- Speed—information can be posted in minutes, which is helpful for crisis communication and corrections.
- The cost of developing and maintaining a site *can* be less than reaching audiences through more traditional media forms. Be sure to factor in content development, hosting, and site maintenance.
- Unlimited availability: The home page is available 24 hours a day, 365 days a year—assuming that the host is operating. This allows direct, unmediated access to audiences.
- The potential for more detailed information on message tracking.
- Comprehensive systems can reach multiple audiences. Managers are developing systems that distinguish between users who are consumers, members of the media, general browsers, or competitors, and directing content accordingly. That allows information to be customized for particular target audiences. For example, a home page might allow reporters to request the automatic distribution of a company's new product releases in the form most useful to them (fax, E-mail, U.S. Postal Service mail, etc.). A reporter can receive exactly the information he or she wants in a timely fashion, in the most useful form. This helps the manager function as a facilitator.
- Interactive tools can make Web sites more useful to audiences than more traditional public relations resources.

Hypertext and links give users a starting point for contacting a variety of sources.

Site Planning

Site planning begins with knowing exactly what you want the site to do. These goals will drive both site content and structure.

"Establish clear goals and objectives for the Web site," according to Diane Witmer, author of *Spinning the Web*. "Write down a goal: *Why* are you developing this site?"[7] The next step is a site map. "This means figuring out what components you want to include, which audience will access each of the components, and determining how you want them to be connected."[8] Diagrams and flow charts help make the plan real.

The manager must think of new and innovative approaches to the site to take full advantage of the Internet. "Just as organizations have learned that it takes more than posting their news releases to establish productive and substantive on-line relationships with the media, it will take more than posting the corporate brochure on your Web site to engage consumers," advises Debbie Neville of the high-tech agency O'Keeffe & Company, Inc. "To 'experience' information is an infinitely more compelling, persuasive, even entertaining means of communicating." She predicts that

> the opportunity for interaction will continue to shape an increasingly high level of expectation on the part of Internet users, requiring that an organization's Web site, to be competitive, be more interesting for the Web visitor.[9]

When the plan is in place, the manager must determine who will be responsible for building the site. Some managers learn code or use site-building templates to design the site themselves. Some outsource the entire project; many contract out the mechanics but develop and control the content.

6.2: Creating a Press-Friendly Web Site

Facilitating media support is one of the most important goals of the public relations manager. To ensure that your company's site helps you help the press, follow these strategies from Debbie Neville of the high-tech agency O'Keeffe & Company, Inc:

Make sure the press can find your site.

If possible, a Web site name should be the company or organization's name followed by ".com" or ".org." Most reporters will try this before using search engines. Try to register all possible names for your company. Make sure your meta tags include critical key words for your organization, and ensure that your home page title includes both your company name and major category. In addition, include your Web site address on everything—business cards, product literature, press releases, E-mail signatures, etc.

Organize site information based on the tasks of your visitors. Reporters will turn to your site if they find information quickly and easily. Provide a link directly from the home page entitled "Press Information," which will lead to appropriate media contacts, press releases, success stories, and a calendar of the organization's upcoming events.

Keep it brief. The home page should be simple, composed of a brief explanation of the organization (and a telephone number) with clearly labeled section headings, such as, "About the Company," "History," "Products and Services," "Contact Information," "Press Information," and "Site Map."

Serve as an information resource. Include white papers written by company executives and industry analysts, links to research on your industry, and links to appropriate industry organizations. Offer value-added content beyond marketing rhetoric.

Include downloadable artwork. Photography can increase the amount of space devoted to your story and adds an element of visual interest, thus increasing retention.

Enable interaction. When appropriate, include a product

demonstration. Perhaps a video clip of a customer talking about the results they have achieved with your product, or a "request an interview/request a product to review" form.

Include a press guest book. Invite reporters to register on-line to be included on the press list. Keep the request form brief to encourage reporters to take the time to reply: Include fields for name, outlet, phone, fax, and E-mail.

Revise and refresh. If the last release on your site is dated six months ago, your corporate image will be stagnant. Ensure that releases are posted and that corporate product information is updated.*

---

*Excerpted from Neville, Debbie, "Creating a Press-Friendly Web Site," *Public Relations Tactics*, December 1999.

Site Development and Maintenance

An argument against reliance on an external webmaster comes from Mike Crawford, president of Dallas-based MC Communications, a high-tech specialty firm: "That would be like turning over a public relations plan to a computer programmer. What's a Web master except an engineer who has learned the programming it takes to create an on-line presence? Do they really know about public relations?"[10]

Even if managers outsource only the mechanics, they must learn to write for the web. This requires a succinct style and an openness to take advantage of the various distinct benefits of the medium, in particular, looking for opportunities to employ links, audio and video clips, and interactive tools to take the presentation beyond traditional text. The Web site must reinforce existing programs; its messages, graphic packages, logos, and other elements must be consistent with print materials.

"Small things overlooked at this stage can become technical and maintenance nightmares," Witmer cautions. She suggests, for example, that if you ...

think you may eventually want a full annual report on-line, organize your file directories to accommodate it now, even if this year, you will simply post a one-page text-only profit-and-loss statement. Create separate directories for images, so you won't have image documents cluttering up your server. The better the site and server directories are planned at this point, the easier it will be to update, modify, and expand in the future."[11]

Don't forget to plan and staff for support—for the expected and the exceptional. "Well-designed Web sites incorporate two-way communication between the client and visitors to the site," Witmer explains:

> This means the client must have the resources to respond efficiently and effectively to a potentially large volume of E-mail inquiries. All too often, clients find themselves bombarded with more E-mail than they can possibly handle. If the client cannot respond to E-mail quickly, the Web site will do more public relations harm than good.[12]

Site Management

When the site "goes live," managers must motivate audiences to use it.

The site name is important—get it right and draw the appropriate audiences, get it wrong and no one will be able to find it; or, worse, it will be confused with sites related to irrelevant subjects. Consider registering the site under a number of similar domain names to capture users who might be guessing at the name.

A number of low-cost services register domain names, or a site manager can file a domain name by contacting InterNIC, <www.netsol.com>, the cooperative organization that serves as a depository for domain names.

The next step is to get the site's address into the appropriate databases and search engines. Cross-list the site with affinity links and take advantage of high-traffic, general-interest portals that critique and direct other sites, funneling traffic toward the best options in a particular category.

Get feedback on-line through on-line chats, bulletin boards, and interactive mechanisms. These forums can be part of your site or industry or professional sites.

When the site is bug-free and letter perfect, market it, and use it aggressively. Refer reporters, clients, and prospective clients to it as often as possible. Include the address on all printed materials, including press releases, business cards, and letterhead. If the site is organized, easily navigated, current, and informative, audiences will be back to use it again. Include a "bookmark" function allowing users to store the site address for easier access.

Other Distribution Technologies

A Web site is only one way to distribute information. Public relations managers should also consider video news releases (VNRs), teleconferencing systems, and CD-ROMs.

VNRs

The use of video news releases (VNRs) has grown approximately 25 percent per year in the 1990s. VNRs distribute messages to the broadcast media in the form shown on the air, increasing control by the practitioner and acceptance by broadcasters. Creative managers use VNRs for non-media audiences as well; in annual reports, employee newsletters, and other forms of controlled communication.

Teleconferencing

Teleconferencing includes video conferencing, audio conferencing, and groupware, a software system allowing multiple computer users to simultaneously work together on different documents. Initial system costs for teleconferencing have dropped dramatically, but they still remain relatively high: a desktop unit costs as much as $55,000.

6.3: Satellite Media Tours

Satellite Media Tours, or SMTs, have taken off in the past decade. Author Katie Sweeney provides a series of tips for how to make them work for your clients:

> With so many SMTs out there these days, booking one isn't easy. TV stations are getting choosier, and they're increasingly savvy to overly commercial messages. If a story doesn't have genuine news value, or the spokesperson isn't a national authority, it's tough to find airtime.

Her solution? Make the location interesting to improve your chances of getting the story booked, and make sure that the location is the appropriate match for the product.

To extend the reach of the SMT, Sweeney recommends distributing it on-line. "Many providers say they're already streaming some video and audio onto company Web sites, although they admit the technology isn't perfect yet,"[*] she writes. She also notes that the production session can be used as an opportunity for an Internet chat, although there are technical limitations with end-users that can limit this approach.

Faster and more reliable transmissions are making SMTs more popular every day, but as the technology behind satellite media tours improves, design and application innovation increases as well. Public relations managers should be as creative as possible in developing unique and useful content and then discovering novel approaches to distributing this communication.

---

[*]Excerpted from Sweeney, Katie, "SMTs are Booming, but Tougher to Book," *Public Relations Tactics*, July 2000.

One alternative is public retail video conferencing, in which organizations rent two or more spaces and connecting communications equipment for approximately $300 per hour.

Improvements such as ISDN lines for better picture quality have led to more creative uses of teleconferencing, as practitioners employ them for internal activities (such as discussion sessions among members of a widely dispersed organization) and external activities (such as satellite media tours).

CD-ROMs

The CD-ROM is a relatively inexpensive way to distribute large amounts of information and reach a range of audiences with text, graphics, sight, and sound. Consider these tips from Tony Harrison, Vice President/Client Service Manager at the Idaho marketing firm Oliver, Russell & Associates:

- Start with research. This should also be designed to answer important questions to guide the CD's development: What percentage of your target audience has the hardware required to run a multimedia CD? How many potential recipients are willing to review one? What types of computers and operating systems do your targets have?
- Assemble a winning team. Developing a CD-ROM requires a wide array of skills. You'll need talented copywriters, graphic designers, illustrators, multimedia developers, computer programmers, videographers, photographers, audio engineers, and voice talent, as well as someone who is organized and able to coordinate the team's efforts. Chemistry is important because it might take upwards of a year to complete the CD.
- Focus on your audience.
- Make the CD flexible.
- Create interactive content.

- Use the technology to your advantage by making the CD as interactive as possible.
- Don't be afraid to put a wealth of information on it. CD-ROMs can hold a great deal of data—650MB. If it's intelligently organized, people can access as little or as much information as they desire without any hassles.
- Make it user-friendly. User-friendly interfaces are a must. Make the buttons big and the typography on them large, and use a very readable font. Moreover, CDs should be easy to navigate from screen to screen. Don't create too many layers or levels, and always give people a reference point so they know where they are at all times.
- Arrange your images smartly. If you're dealing with a large amount of still photography and illustrations, have all the images scanned onto photo CDs to make assembling "cast members" an easy task.
- Consider creating an image-placement database. Then, if a photo or illustration that's used in several places needs to be replaced, making substitutions throughout the CD will be a snap.
- Archive each step in the development of graphic images, too. Otherwise, you may be forced to reinvent the wheel if, for instance, an image you created in Illustrator, touched up in Photoshop, and saved as a PICT file has a typo.
- Get rid of bugs in the system. Test your CD on the worst-case-scenario machine, because it will behave differently on various computers. Multimedia developers tend to have high-performance, state-of-the-art work stations, and you want to ensure the CD will perform satisfactorily on a computer with only the minimum system requirements.
- Update periodically. Don't view your CD-ROM as a one-shot project, but rather as an evolutionary process. CDs should be updated periodically to keep their contents current.[13]

Conclusions

New technologies will not replace the traditional tools of public relations, but the fast-paced growth in information and technology—and thus, the expectations for both—is creating tremendous pressure on public relations managers to increase their use of emerging systems. Many of these technologies are becoming mandatory in the public relations industry; managers must address the budget and planning issues associated with these commitments.

Amid this pressure and continuing developments, public relations managers should remember that their job is not simply acquiring the latest software or hardware, but identifying which functions are most useful to help collect, package, and distribute information. The challenge for managers is to determine the short-term and long-term needs of their organizations and weigh the overall costs and benefits of these evolving technologies while continuing to operate in an exceptionally dynamic atmosphere for clients, audiences, and members of the media.

Action Plan

Conduct an "internal technology audit" in your organization. Identify the hardware and software, as well as the technological capabilities of the staff. Divide the audit into three sections: information gathering, packaging, and distributing. Grade each area and determine the best way to improve the systems.

Conduct a similar audit for your key clients. Meet with your clients to discuss technology, and determine how well your computer equipment "talks" to theirs. Identify gaps and limitations as well as technology and training solutions.

Conduct another audit with the most important members of the media.

Based on your findings from the three audits, answer the following questions: What information do people need? In what form do they need it? What is needed, in terms of technology and training, to improve the process?

Exercises

No. 1: Find Brilliance in Others

Here is an opportunity to challenge the sophistication of your colleagues while tapping into their expertise. At the next gathering (professional or otherwise), ask each to identify the single best piece of technology (hardware or software) that he or she has learned about in the past year. Ask for specific applications of the technology and benefits that came from it.

No. 2: Avoid the Junk

Reverse the process of Exercise 1 and ask your colleagues for examples of technologies that have disappointed them. From grandiose sales pitches to bug-filled software, there are plenty of products out there that you should try to avoid. Learn from the mistakes of others—this can save you time, money, and embarrassment.

No. 3: What Works on the Web

If your organization has a Web site, find out how to make it more useful to your audiences. Conduct a survey or focus group with primary users of the site. Determine what other sites they use and why they turn to them. Revisit your site regularly from the perspective of your audience to make sure that it does what *they* want it to do.

CHAPTER 7

Legal Issues

I am not determining a point of law; I am restoring tranquility.
—Edmund Burke

Introduction

While most public relations organizations have access to legal counsel, it is still important for the manager to be familiar with the law in several key areas. By familiarizing themselves with this information, managers will better understand their legal rights and responsibilities, avoid some actions that could lead to lawsuits or threats of lawsuits, and be prepared to work with the organization's legal counsel.

This chapter focuses on legal information in the areas most frequently addressed by a public relations manager. These include laws related to mass media, corporate political speech, defamation, copyright, trademark, privacy, appropriation, distorted/fictional portrayals, and physical/technological intrusion. The chapter also highlights the differences and similarities between public relations and legal perspectives. However, the public relations manager should also appreciate the distinction between what is legal and what is ethical. Lawyers and public relations managers often work in gray areas, forced to make high-stakes decisions in high-pressure environments. It can be tempting to rationalize ethically questionable choices by defining a course of action as legal, customary, or justifiable under specific circumstances. PR managers, like lawyers, represent not only their clients but also their professions, and should strive to adhere to the highest standards of conduct. The ethical issues discussed in the next chapter will facilitate a more thorough understanding, of legal issues in the public relations profession as well as other ethical concerns.

Similar Goals, Different Tactics

On the surface, it may appear that the public relations manager and the lawyer have a lot in common. Both are looking out for their clients' best interests—in fact, they have a fiduciary requirement to do so. Both are legally and ethically bound to tell the truth. Both conduct research to develop positions that present their clients favorably. But the two professionals are usually addressing different audiences, and it is at that point that the strategic approaches of the two professions begin to differ.

The lawyer focuses on the audience in a court of law: primarily the judge and, when present, the jury. A public relations manager, on the other hand, focuses on several audiences: internal audiences, such as employees of a company, stockholders, and suppliers; as well as external audiences, such as government regulators, and, of course, the client's customers.

Because the audiences differ, the professional strategies differ. The lawyer will tend to reveal information only as a last resort, to avoid providing ammunition to opposing counsel. The lawyer must consider the possibility that any statement made on the client's behalf could become part of a deposition or lawsuit. Even if information isn't used in a particular legal maneuver, it can be an indication of a legal strategy. Why risk tipping your hand?

The public relations manager, on the other hand, is trained to get the message out first as a way of framing the issue. While most lawyers have no problem issuing a "no comment" to the press (an audience that is rarely their central concern), the public relations manager considers a press inquiry another opportunity to communicate with multiple audiences, many of whom may be key to the organization's success. Press relations are just one area where these fundamentally different philosophies play out.

Clients often need both legal and public relations counsel. When the two clash, which one wins? More often than not, the lawyers—for two reasons:

1. The legal profession is usually held in higher regard than the public relations profession.
2. Situations involving lawyers may include immediate downsides that must be addressed; product liability lawsuits and jail sentences get anyone's attention.

Addressing issues solely from a legal perspective can be extremely damaging in the long term, however. The approach can produce a classic case of winning the battle but losing the war. It is the job of public relations managers to remind their clients that legal action can result in irreparable damage to relationships with key constituents.

How does the public relations manager command the same respect as legal counsel? One way is to begin working with the CEO long before legal complications are underway. Emphasize the potential downsides of failing to address issues from a public relations perspective in the same way that a lawyer might—in terms of economic liability. The damages that loom are relationships with key constituents, along with potential financial losses that could be as large as any jury award.

Public relations managers can also raise their profiles by initiating dialogue with their company's legal department before a legal situation occurs. Establish a relationship with counsel that recognizes the values and priorities of each party. If a public relations manager is willing to learn why a lawyer won't talk to the press before an Initial Public Offering or a liability suit, perhaps the lawyer can learn the value of substituting a carefully prepared statement for the traditional "no

7.1: Lawyers are Learning the Art of Media Relations

Does William Ginsburg give too many interviews? Should a media relations specialist be part of a high-profile court case? Richard Stack, a PR professor at American University, former public defender and author of *"Courts, Counselor, and Correspondents: A Media Relations Analysis of the Legal System,* offers his opinion in this interview with *Public Relations Tactics* Editor-in-Chief John Elsasser:

Besides football players and cops, attorneys used to give the worst sound bites. However, attorneys seem to understand the importance of media relations these days.
Robert Shapiro was one of the leaders. He produced several articles about the need to appear more public-friendly. There's a phrase I like: The opening statement before the opening statement. The media makes the opening statement. Where do jurors come from? The public. You want the public to have a positive impression of your client. Attorneys have begun to realize the significance of the court of public opinion. It's been more recently that lawyers have taken it so seriously, especially with the proliferation of the media.

Then there's William Ginsburg, an attorney who doesn't know how to turn down an interview. Is there a danger in talking with the press too much?
A lawyer needs to conduct his or her media relations judiciously. There's a danger of getting burned by overexposure. I think that's what has happened in Ginsburg's case. The public has perceived this guy as a media hound. It has not served his client, Monica Lewinsky, very well at all.

Perhaps Ginsburg was just bucking for a job as a network commentator. Many of his peers have become news commentators.
I believe there's a place for that—as long as they're not the attorney of record on a case. There needs to be better professional relations between lawyers and journalists for the sake of the public. I put PR practitioners in the equation as well because they're often the intermediary between attorneys and reporters. The end result of solid working relationships between these three groups of professionals would be more accurate and objective court stories. The public would be the ultimate beneficiary of that. We would have a more informed citizenry. And that's what a good, active democracy is based on.

More attorneys are getting media relations help on cases. However, there's a stigma that "only the guilty need public relations." What's your take?
Attorneys are beginning to realize that to provide full service to their clients, they need to represent them not only in the court of law, but in the court of public opinion. While legal opinions are rendered in a court of law, personal reputation—sometimes even public policy—is made in the court of public opinion. It's important to preserve one's integrity and long-term reputation, so an attorney really does have to do battle in the court of public opinion for the client. I also have a different outlook: At this point, it's something only for the wealthy.

PR counsel does not come cheap. I say what's good for the rich ought to be good for the poor. We should be training more public communications students to engage in litigation public relations so that a public law firm—or the public defender's office, legal aid offices, American Civil Liberties Union offices—could also have the benefit of their expertise.*

---

*Elsasser, John, "Lawyers are Learning the Art of Public Relations" *Public Relations Tactics*, June 1998.

comment." Make it a priority to find common ground that allows both sides to meet some of their goals. Develop guidelines for both departments to follow when action from both is required.

Despite a history of antagonism, the relationship between legal and public relations counsel is not doomed to eternal conflict. As media coverage of legal proceedings has become more prevalent, lawyers have begun to understand the value of obtaining solid media training—for themselves as well as for their clients.

How Mass Media Law Applies to Public Relations

Who and what are covered by laws related to public relations? The First Amendment to the Constitution states:

> Congress shall make no law respecting an establishment of religion, or prohibiting the free exercise thereof; or abridging the freedom of speech, or of the press; or the right of the people peaceably to assemble; and to petition the Government for a redress of grievances.

While the First Amendment appears to be all-inclusive and unambiguous, the application of the amendment is far more nuanced and complicated and is always applied in the context of other parts of the constitution. The First Amendment applies to public relations issues from libel to privacy to copyright, so the PR manager should be familiar with a wide range of issues reflecting freedom of speech and freedom of the press.

Different Media, Different Rights

Since this amendment was adopted in 1781, however, U.S. courts have issued a wide range of rulings indicating that freedom of speech is anything but universal. Freedom of speech is conditional. The amendment protects some kinds of speech more than it protects others. For example, print media such as newspapers and magazines enjoy stronger legal protection than broadcast media such as radio and television. Broadcast media operate on airwaves that are considered public property, so these media are subject to additional regulation. In the last decade, this legal distinction has come under review in the courts because increased channel capacity may negate the so-called "limited spectrum" argument. Differences in regulation between media have also become more complicated with the merger of traditional forms and introduction of new forms of media. For example, the courts continue to grapple with legal protection for content transmitted over the Internet.

So far, the courts have treated the Internet more like a print medium than a broadcast medium, providing significant First Amendment protection to individuals and organizations using this medium. While the Internet's distribution system bears more resemblance to broadcast than to print, the limited spectrum argument does not yet apply to the new medium due to its unlimited potential for expansion.

The Right to Collect and Distribute Information

Public relations managers have limited legal leverage in using the First Amendment to gather information, because U.S. courts do not recognize this as an explicit right. For example, public access to government meetings and records is primarily the result of federal and state statutes such as the Freedom of Information Act (1966) and the Government in Sunshine Act (1976). *Richmond Newspapers, Inc. v. Virginia* (1980) recognized the right of access to court proceedings, with some limitations.

Public relations managers, like members of the media, have more powerful First Amendment rights when it comes to distributing information.

Consumers have the right to receive some forms of both advertising communication (*Virginia State Board of Pharmacy v. Virginia*

7.2: Access to
Federal Information and Meetings

What leverage does a public relations manager have when seeking information?

For government records, the best leverage comes from the Freedom of Information Act (FOIA)—for meetings, look to the Government in Sunshine Act.

Adopted by Congress in 1966, the FOIA was designed to provide access to records generated by the federal government. These records include paper documents, film, tapes, and physical evidence in criminal prosecutions. The act was substantially strengthened in 1995, when then-President Clinton signed an executive order that loosened secrecy rules in the executive branch and extended the records to include electronic data.

Any member of the press or public may make an FOIA request. But the FOIA process can be complicated and time-consuming, and should generally be used only after other approaches have failed. When seeking federal information, it is best to start with an informal request or a review of public court records; these can often produce the information in less time. Federal agencies frequently disregard their obligation to respond to an FOIA request within ten days. Requests may also be blocked if the data involve any of these exempted categories:

1. National security
2. "Housekeeping" materials, such as internal personnel rules
3. Material exempted by statute
4. Trade secrets
5. Working papers/lawyer-client privilege
6. Personal privacy (personnel and medical files, for example)
7. Law enforcement records
8. Financial institutions
9. Geological data

> ### Open-Meeting Laws
> Let the sun shine in! Since 1976, the Government in Sunshine Act
> has opened meetings of more than fifty federal boards to the pub-
> lic and required those boards to post notice of their meetings at
> least a week in advance. Public relations managers should note,
> however, that this same law bars informal communication
> between agency officials and individuals or company representa-
> tives who might have business with the agency unless that com-
> munication is recorded and added to the public record.
>
> Some meetings are exempt from the Sunshine Act. These
> include the kinds of exemptions generated by the Freedom of Infor-
> mation Act, as well as meetings concerning arbitration or disposition
> of a particular case.

Citizens Consumer Council, Inc. 1930 [1976]) and corporate communication (*First National Bank of Boston v. Bellotti* [1978]).

Some First Amendment rights work against public relations
practitioners by providing additional protection to the media. For
example, in the case of *Miami Herald Publishing Co. v. Tornillo* (1974),
the Supreme Court found that a private newspaper could not be
forced to publish news stories, advertisements, letters, or even replies
to letters. This protection was extended to public utilities a decade
later, when the court ruled that a gas and electric company was protected from having to carry the message of a consumer group in the
company's billing envelopes (*Pacific Gas & Elec. Co. v. Public Utilities
Commission* [1986]).

Corporate Political Speech

Public relations managers frequently represent corporations, so they
should understand the First Amendment rights of those legal entities.
In political speech, including participation in referenda and elections,
the rights of corporations are different from the rights of individuals.

The Supreme Court has supported the nearly unlimited right of corporations to participate in referenda, in which citizens vote on specific propositions (*First National Bank of Boston v. Bellotti* [1978]). The courts have also ruled that organizations, including public utilities, have the right to distribute information to citizens—as well as the right to decline distribution of information. Furthermore, corporations have the right to communicate to publics about issues other than those that directly affect their business.

7.3: Access to
State Information and Meetings

There are nearly as many rules about access to state information and meetings as there are states.

State open-records laws normally apply to mostly state, city, county, township, and village agencies: commissions, boards, bureaus, divisions, departments, school districts, public utilities, and municipal corporations. In most states, open records laws do not apply to the courts, legislature, or governor's office. In every state, if you have the right to access a record, you have the right to copy that record.

Open-meeting rules vary from extremely strong access (Florida and Tennessee) to very limited (Pennsylvania). Even when the laws favor access, state legislators frequently exempt themselves from such regulation. In addition, meetings normally subject to access laws may be closed for executive sessions.

What if a citizen is barred from a public meeting or a meeting is held without notice? Half the statutes provide for criminal penalties and, in many states, any action taken at the meetings is null and void if citizens are illegally stopped from attending.

If you are denied access to a meeting you believe you are entitled to attend, do not leave until you are ordered to do so. If so ordered, identify the person making the request and ask for a legal basis for the action.

For three decades, corporate rights to political speech in elections were determined primarily by the Federal Election Campaign Act of 1971. The ability of individuals and corporations to contribute to candidates and political parties changed dramatically in 2002, however, when Congress passed and President George W. Bush signed the Bipartisan Campaign Reform Act.

There are three areas of the bill that the PR manager should be aware of:

1. *Limitations on "Hard Money"*: The bill still allows individuals to contribute up to $5,000 per year to a single Political Action Committee, or PAC. However, it raises the limit on individual contributions to candidates from $1,000 per election (or $2,000 counting both primary and general elections) to $2,000 ($4,000 primary and general) for presidential and Senate candidates. The annual contribution limit is now $25,000 for national parties and $10,000 for state parties. All the new levels, except for state parties, are indexed for inflation adjustment. The bill also raises the annual aggregate total an individual can contribute to candidates, PACs, and parties from $25,000 per year ($50,000 per 2-year cycle) to $95,000 per cycle. Of this amount, up to $37,500 may go to candidates and $57,500 to national and state parties and PACs (but not more than $37,500 to the state parties and PACs).

2. *Elimination of "Soft Money"*: The bill prohibits corporations and unions from spending treasury money on pre-election TV or radio so-called "issue ads" that are, in effect, ads advocating one candidate over another. This includes broadcast ads that refer to a clearly identified federal candidate within thirty days of a primary or sixty days of a general election and that are directed at members of the candidate's electorate. The corporate ban also encompasses certain nonprofit groups, including 501c4 advocacy and 527 political organizations.

3. *Disclosure*: The bill requires any individual or group who spends more than $10,000 on such communications in a

year to publicly disclose its identity, place of business and contributors of $1,000 or more. This requirement does not apply to corporations or unions. It also requires disclosure for donations over $200 to presidential inaugural committees, public access to broadcasters' records of political advertisements, clearer sponsor identification for election advertising and more rapid public disclosure of pre-election "independent expenditures" expressly advocating the election or defeat of a candidate (including identification of the donors).

Political communication regulations for both referenda and elections may change rapidly. Support for corporate speech related to referenda remains tenuous for two reasons. First, the support is frequently discussed in the context of its contribution to the democratic process, and should the speech be found to threaten that process, corporate rights may be restricted. Second, these rights have emerged though cases with slim majorities and strong dissents.

As for corporate speech related to elections, the ink had barely dried on the Bipartisan Campaign Reform Act before a number of individuals and organizations were in court arguing against the constitutionality of the bill. While a number of major components of the bill may eventually be revised, the act still provides the best contemporary legal guidelines on corporate participation in the election process.

Defamation

Defamation can take two forms: libel and slander. Defamation that is written or appears in print is libel. Defamation that is spoken is slander. Broadcast defamation, which occurs more rarely than print defamation, is usually classified as libel. The distinction between libel and slander is important because a plaintiff in a slander suit must prove a more precise level of damages than a plaintiff in a libel suit and because, historically, slander suits produce smaller damage awards than libel suits.

Defamation law is a complicated patchwork of statutes and court rulings on both state and federal levels. The PRSA Code of Professional Standards defines defamation as communication that tends to "diminish the respect, good will, confidence, or esteem in which (a person) is held, or to excite adverse or unpleasant feeling about him."[1]

The last two decades have seen an increase in the number of defamation suits filed—and in the time taken to resolve them. In

---

7.4: Libel and the Internet

Does libel apply on the Internet? If so, who is liable?

In recent cases, the courts have ruled that defamation on the Internet is libel rather than slander.

In 1991, a U.S. District Court in New York determined that CompuServe was not responsible in a defamation case in which the company transmitted a gossip column (*Cubby, Inc. v. CompuServe, Inc.* [1991]). The court ruled that CompuServe had no opportunity to review the material before transmitting it and did not have reason to know about the defamation.

On the other hand, the Supreme Court of the same state ruled in 1995 that Prodigy Services Company, another distributor of on-line information, *was* liable for defamation after transmitting information on an on-line bulletin board (*Stratton Oakmont, Inc. v. Prodigy Services* [1995]).

The difference? In the latter case, the judge found that Prodigy had promoted itself as an on-line service that monitored material on the network and thus acted more like a publisher than a simple distributor, with the attendant greater responsibility. While this area of the law continues to evolve, wise public relations managers will err on the side of caution, treating any on-line activity the same as any other written form of public communication.

7.5: Your Company was Slammed! Should You Sue?

You wake up one day to find an extremely negative story about your company on the front page of the business section. Your first reaction is to dial your lawyer. Before you pick up the phone, however, consider the following:

1. Libel suits can drain your organization of time and money. Legal fees are just the start of it. Consider the whole cost, factor in resources you will need to expend preparing for the case.
2. You have the burden of proof.
3. If the story concerns a mistake made by your organization, it won't necessarily be considered defamation. News organizations have argued successfully that readers of a story that reports a single error by an organization do not necessarily think less of the organization—in effect, everyone makes mistakes.
4. Finally, and perhaps most important, remember that any case you initiate may become news in itself—and that's usually bad news for you. Media coverage of your suit will inevitably include summaries of facts of the case and repetition of the allegation that brought you into court. When Texas cattlemen accused Oprah Winfrey of violating food disparagement laws in 1998, nearly every report on the case included a reference to her statements about the detrimental qualities of meat. Some vegetarian groups even used the publicity to further their anti-beef positions. The nuance of your case—including whether you win or lose—may be lost on key audiences.

There are certainly cases where a libel suit is legitimate and should be pursued. Sure, you would love to see the look on that reporter's face when the jury announces a multimillion-dollar award in your favor, but that's not likely to happen. What *is* likely is that, win

> or lose, you and your organization will be dealing with many of the negative ramifications of deciding to initiate the suit.
>
> If you are certain that a negative story about your organization is untrue, take a deep breath when you pick up the phone to call your lawyer. Many times, a call to the reporter (or the reporter's boss), in which you point out the inaccuracy and ask for a correction, may be the better management decision.

libel cases, the *average* jury award in the 1990s was more than a million dollars; the average cost of defending a libel suit, including those that didn't go to trial, was $100,000. Beyond the potential financial negatives of defamation are professional and ethical problems. Even when public relations managers are found not guilty in a defamation lawsuit, the allegation can permanently stain their image.

While defamation cases are most often brought against members of the media, public relations managers are also vulnerable. Nearly every form of communication used in public relations may be subject to laws in this area. These include press releases, photographs, brochures, posters, internal and external newsletters, slide shows, videotapes, and speeches.

Two of the most important resources for a public relations manager are time and money. Both can be rapidly consumed when the manager is charged with defamation—regardless of whether the allegation ever leads to a legal case or comes to trial.

Most people and organizations can sue for defamation. The only people who can't sue for defamation are dead people and criminals whose reputations are so notorious that courts will not accept their cases. No person can sue for damage to the reputation of another. The only organizations that can't sue for defamation are government entities, such as cities, or large, generic groups based only on such common characteristics as ethnicity or political beliefs. Individual businesses, nonprofit organizations, labor unions, and charities can all bring defamation suits.

7.6: Who's a Public Figure?

The issue of "public" versus "private" people is crucial in libel cases. A plaintiff who is a public person must prove, in addition to the standard elements of libel, that the defendant acted with "actual malice." Actual malice is the act of publishing while knowing that the libelous statement is false, or with reckless disregard for whether it is true.

What makes an individual a public person? Most people would agree that the president of the United States is a public figure, but what about the president of your organization? What about *you*?

Some identifications are simple. Any person *elected* to government office is a public official and, therefore, a public figure. The courts have also determined that any government employee who has, or appears to have, substantial responsibility for the conduct of governmental affairs, or who plays a role in developing public policy, is also a public official. However, that person must hold a position that would invite public scrutiny independent of the exposure a person would receive related to the libel case.

As if that doesn't make the definition complicated enough, remember that most libel law is developed at the state level, creating fifty different standards. And that's just for public *officials*.

For public *figures*, the Supreme Court divides citizens into all-purpose and limited-purpose, although both must adhere to the actual malice standard in a libel suit. All-purpose public figures are persons who "occupy positions of such pervasive power and influence that they are deemed public figures for all purposes,"* according to Supreme Court Justice Lewis Powell. Powell classifies limited-purpose public figures as those who have "thrust themselves to the forefront of particular public controversies in order to influence the resolution of the issues involved."† If a person does not seek public attention, he or she is not likely to be considered a public figure, even if accidentally or unwillingly introduced into a controversial situation.

So, would that include the CEO of your organization? That

depends on the size of the organization, the amount of media coverage it has received, and the public position of the executive, both within the industry and within the community.

Businesses, like individuals, can be classified as public figures. However, the distinction between all-purpose and limited-purpose classifications becomes more complicated because businesses advertise products, interact at various times with government organizations, and distribute goods locally as well as nationally.

If you find these definitions difficult to apply, you are not alone. Since Powell first made the distinction in 1974, courts at the state and federal level have grappled to clarify the differences.

Gertz v. Robert Welch, Inc., 418 U.S. 323 (1974).
†Ibid.

While many defamation cases are legitimate, some may be filed—or threatened—strictly to harass or intimidate a speaker, to drain resources from an adversary, or even to chill individual or media discussion of an organization. However, parties that use the legal system for frivolous complaints or intimidation expose themselves to potential countersuits by defendants.

The Roles of Plaintiffs and Defendants

The initial burden of proof in a defamation suit is on the plaintiff, or person bringing the case. A libel case plaintiff must prove the following elements:

1. that the libel has been published (disseminated)
2. that the defamation involves the plaintiff (plaintiff identified)
3. that the material is defamatory
4. that the material is false

5. that the defendant is at fault
6. that the defamation resulted in personal harm (loss of reputation, emotional distress, or loss of business revenues)

The burden of proof in a defamation suit rests largely on the plaintiff's status in the community. If the plaintiff is considered a private individual, there is a lower standard for fault. If the person is a public figure or public official, however, he or she must prove actu-

---

7.7: What's the Damage?

If you lose a libel case, how much will it cost you?

The answer comes in four forms of damages: special, actual, presumed, and punitive. Each covers different kinds of harm and requires different burdens of proof by the plaintiff.

Special damages are exact monetary damages, money that a plaintiff can prove he or she lost as a result of the libel, and are limited to financial loss.

Actual damages include out-of-pocket loss or money loss (which can be relatively easily determined) as well as damages for "actual harm inflicted by defamatory falsehood (which) include impairment of reputation and standing in the community, personal humiliation and mental anguish and suffering,"* (which can be more difficult to determine).

Presumed damages, also known as general or compensatory damages, may be awarded to a plaintiff without proof of injury or harm.

Punitive damages, or exemplary damages, are designed to punish the defendant for misconduct rather than simply compensate the plaintiff for injury. These are the most feared damages, because there is no upper limit on such judgments and they tend to be large awards.

Gertz v. Robert Welch, Inc., 418 U.S. 323 (1974).

al malice. Be aware that states have different standards. Public relations managers should familiarize themselves with the standards of the state in which they work.

Defending Yourself in a Defamation Suit

A defamation defense is based on the strongest elements of the case in any or all of four areas: consent, truth, qualified privilege, and fair comment. While each defense may seem clear and distinct, there are ambiguities and caveats to each.

Consent

That extra client review of a document that seems like such a time-consuming waste may someday be the key to a libel defense. If a person approves an article written about him, he cannot sue the writer for libel when the article is published.

Truth

Truth would appear to be the simplest and strongest defense. Demonstrate that what you have written or said is accurate, and the plaintiff's case collapses. However, the concept of truth can be ambiguous in the courtroom and public relations managers must be aware of the nuances of this defense.

For example, the truth defense is strengthened if the manager can demonstrate that his or her actions adhered to the standards of the profession. The combination of true statements and conduct reflecting the accepted practices of the public relations industry makes for a strong defense.

Second, a statement may be accurate but still not true. For example, if a manager included defamatory quotes from someone in a press release, it would be accurate that the person said it, but the public relations manager could still be sued for libel if the statements were false.

Finally, and most important, truth is an elusive concept—what may be factually correct may also lead to misconception, and the courts may emphasize what the average consumer of the information might interpret it to mean rather than stress a literal interpretation of the words.

Qualified Privilege

Absolute qualified privilege is reserved primarily for individuals who are working for the government and acting in their official capacities, such as judges or public information officers, or for statements made or documents filed during legal proceedings. Public relations managers are not entitled to this defense. They may, however, assert qualified privilege, which allows anyone to publish a report on a public document or the proceedings of a public meeting as long as that report is fair and accurate.

Fair Comment

Fair comment allows for publication or broadcast of opinions regarding people operating in the public sphere. Although this area of libel law is undergoing significant changes, most judges evaluate a fair comment defense according to three criteria:

1. whether the comment is an opinion
2. whether the subject is one of legitimate public interest
3. if the opinion focuses on an individual, whether the comment deals with public rather than private issues related to that individual

Ownership of Creative Work:
Copyright, Trademark, and Servicemark

When a public relations manager authorizes a writer to produce a brochure and a graphic artist to design it, who owns the rights to the work when the piece is done? And for how long?

This part of public relations is covered by copyright law designed to protect creative work. This law is divided into copyright, trademark, and servicemark.

Copyright law provides the owner of a work exclusive control over the use of that work, including the right to reproduce, copy, distribute, display or adapt it. Trademark law protects words, symbols, or designs that identify it as a source of goods and differentiate the company or its product from that of its competitors. Servicemark law, similar to trademark law, protects the distinguishing words, symbols and designs used to differentiate services. In this chapter, the term *trademark* refers to both trademark and servicemark.

While copyright law can be as complex as defamation law, it does have one distinct advantage: laws protecting creative works are enacted at the federal level and, therefore, are consistent throughout the country. In fact, more than 120 countries have agreed to standardize copyright law, so that the law discussed in this chapter applies to most other industrialized nations and to cyberspace as well to as the United States.

Copyright

Copyright covers fixed, tangible forms of expression, including literary works, pictorial and graphic works, motion pictures, newsletters, annual reports, books, newspaper articles, software, advertisements, E-mail, and sound recordings. A work becomes fixed at the point that it is created or recorded so that it can be perceived—words written on paper, film exposed, graphic designs saved on a computer hard drive. The copyright protects the expression of ideas and facts, rather than the facts themselves. Federal documents cannot be copyrighted and are entirely in the public domain.

Copyrights are owned by the work's author or authors, unless the work was created for hire. A coauthor may authorize use of a work without permission from the other author or authors so long as all authors receive royalties. When a work is made for hire, the copyright is owned by the party who hires someone to create the work.

PR managers should be sure to include the exact term "work-for-hire" when writing a contract with a freelancer, so that there is no

7.8: How to Copyright Your Work

If you are an author, you can protect your work with a copyright in just two steps: (1) include a notice of copyright within the text and (2) register and deposit the material with the Copyright Office.

The first step, notice of copyright, is simple. Insert the notice in a prominent place in your work, such as the page immediately following the title page in a book. The notice of copyright should include the copyright symbol (©) or the word "copyright" followed by the year of the first publication and the owner of the copyright.

Once the work is published, you have three months from the date of publication to obtain formal copyright by registering and depositing the work. Begin by ordering an application for registration for copyright or by downloading the application from the United States Copyright Office ((202) 707-9100) or <www.loc.gov/copyright/>). Submit the completed application to the copyright office along with two copies of the work and the copyright fee. The copyright fee starts at $20.00 and increases based on the size of the work. For specifics on the fee or any other requirements, call (202) 707-3000. The application should be submitted to the following address:

Library of Congress
Copyright Office
101 Independence Avenue, S.E.
Washington, D.C. 20559-6000

question about legal ownership of the final product. Freelance photographers and writers who supply their own tools, work in their own offices, and receive no regular salary or benefits retain the copyright to materials they create for a client, unless the work is "specially ordered or commissioned" and both parties sign a work-for-hire agreement. If not bound by a written contract that includes the term "work-for-hire," freelancers may sell their work to a public relations agency for one-time publication and retain all additional copyright protection. Even this seemingly clear-cut statement has led to legal wrangling, however, as freelancers and their clients have gone to court over what constitutes "one-time publication." It remains unclear whether publishing a work in a single form, such as in a newspaper, is the extent of one-time publication, or whether the right extends to the first publication in other forms by the same company. For example, if a publisher distributes the work in paper form but then reproduces it on-line or in a CD, freelancers argue that the one-time publication agreement has been violated. At this time, if public relations managers think a contracted piece may appear in more than one form, they should state clearly in the contract that "one-time publication" includes the first publication in a variety of formats, then list those formats.

Finally, employers may allow employees to publish or display the works they have created, but they are not legally obligated to do so.

The duration of the copyright protection varies. If the copyright is owned by the creator of the work and was not done for hire, the work is copyrighted until 70 years after the creator's death (50 years after death for works created before 1977). If the work was made for hire, the copyright protection extends 120 years from creation of the material or 95 years from the first publication of the material, whichever occurs first.

Trademark

Trademark is not based on the originality of a work, but on the degree to which the work distinguishes that company or product from others—the distinctiveness of the words, symbol, or design.

The trademark can be exceptionally useful in helping practitioners establish and maintain an identity for a client. The practitioner should use such protected marks carefully and consistently in communication and ensure that the press uses the mark with the same precision. Some corporations, for example, run advertisements in journalism publications that explain which words and phrases are trademarked and how they should be used. The initial trademark registration is for ten years, and the owner may apply for renewal in

7.9: How to Apply for a Trademark

You've developed a great slogan for your client, and you want to protect your creative effort. You need to register for a trademark.

You can apply for a trademark as soon as the mark is used, but that leaves a window of exposure between the date of the application and the date of the official registration. While it is illegal to use the registered trademark symbol (®) before federal notification of registration, many practitioners claim ownership during the interim period by including the registration symbol (™) or words "Trademark Pending" next to the symbol or design.

You may download an application for registration from the U.S. Patent and Trademark Office Web site <www.uspto.gov> or order an application by telephone (800-786-9199 or 703-308-4357). Submit the completed application, a drawing of the mark to be protected, three examples of the actual use of the mark with the related services or goods, and a filing fee of $175 for each class of services or goods to be covered by the trademark.

Successful registration of a trademark provides recorded notice worldwide of a claim of ownership; for additional protection, you may also register the trademark in each state in which it will be used. In most states, this is handled through the secretary of state's office.

Once the application is accepted, include the registered trademark symbol (®) whenever the protected work is used.

ten-year increments. Trademark protection can be extended as long as the mark continues to differentiate the product from its competitors. Trademarks may be lost if the company abandons them or if the protracted term evolves into a generic term. Words such as "thermos," "aspirin," and "escalator" were each once protected by trademarks but have all passed in to common usage.

Privacy

Privacy—the right to be left alone—is a legal concept that frequently coincides with the work of the PR professional. From shielding a client from unwanted media attention to deciding when to use footage of employees in a promotional video, managers must understand their rights and responsibilities when dealing in this delicate area.

The body of privacy law is formed by a combination of state regulation, federal legislation, including the Federal Privacy Act of 1974, and court interpretations of the Constitution, particularly the Fourth Amendment.

There are four major areas of privacy law: appropriation, distorted or fictional portrayal, protection of private facts, and intrusion and trespassing.

Appropriation

Appropriation is the area of privacy law that the public relations practitioner deals with most frequently. A person is liable for invasion of privacy if he appropriates to his own use or benefit the name or likeness of another. The likeness can be in the form of a photograph, a unique phrase or expression, a name, or even a nickname, and includes representations made through the use of sound-alike or look-alike talent. These appropriations may be cause for a lawsuit if they appear in many of the communications tools in public relations and advertising, because they are then being used "for purposes of trade." These appearances include press releases, brochures, press kits, posters, flyers, print advertisements, and broadcast advertisements. Appropriations of incidental references, in which a person happens to be associated with a significant event, are not protected by privacy law and can be used for public relations purposes.

Using an appropriation in a positive way is not an adequate defense for appropriation. You can be sued for invasion of privacy even if you use the likeness in a flattering context, on the grounds that the person pictured could lose potential commercial value based on the use of the image. This latter value is not considered a privacy right, but a property right. Some courts have ruled that individuals who become well-known lose their right to be left alone in public but retain the right to profit from their publicity. An individual's privacy rights end when that person dies, but the commercial value of an individual's publicity rights can be willed to heirs or estates. Interpretations of these rights vary widely from state to state.

The best defense in an appropriation lawsuit is consent. Consent is a contractual agreement between parties regarding the use of the name or likeness. The contract should be written and should identify the parties to the agreement, the scope of the agreement, and the duration of the consent. It should also include the terms of consideration (the payment or compensation made to the person whose likeness is being used and the permission to use it).

Without a statement of consideration and payment for usage, the consent agreement can be revoked. If the consent form is being used exclusively for legal purposes and there is no real negotiation about payment, the public relations manager should still agree to pay one dollar and make the payment—a nominal economic exchange that creates an irrevocable legal contract.

Whenever possible, the public relations manager should obtain the broadest possible release from the subject, in terms of both use of the likeness and duration of the consent. For example, that might include the rights to not only take the photograph but also to alter, copyright, sell, or publish the picture for one hundred years. This provides the strongest possible consent defense.

7.10: Appropriation and Employee Newsletters

So you got great snapshots from the company picnic and the board of directors meeting. Now, can you use them in your monthly newsletter?

It depends on where the publication is going and how you are using it.

The privacy rights of people portrayed in the publication will change depending on the publication's function. Don't assume that because you are photographing employees—even on company property during the workday—you have total rights for distribution.

Generally, the more internal the publication's audience, the better your case. If an employee sues over a photograph that appears in a newsletter circulated entirely within the workforce, you could reasonably argue that (1) there was implied consent on the part of the employee, and (2) the photograph was not being used "for the purposes of trade."

But public relations managers are frequently looking to use their best material in multiple outlets. If your photographer captures that "perfect shot," your first thought may be how many local newspapers might jump at the chance to print it. If an item in an employee publication gets a big response, you might consider reprinting it in a publication you send to stockholders and customers. As the usage moves toward external audiences, your right to reproduce the image decreases.

If an image is going to be used in press releases, advertisements, or other material targeted to external publics, be sure to get the subject to sign a consent form before distribution, and remember that the consent terminates when the employee leaves the company unless you have explicit written consent for a longer period. These same rules apply to other forms of printed materials as well as videotapes and audiotapes.

If the subject of the agreement is less than twenty-one years old, the parent or legal guardian of that person should sign the agreement. If the subject is represented by someone else (for example, an agent representing an athlete), the representative should provide documentation of that authority and sign the consent agreement.

Sometimes members of the media cite newsworthiness as a privacy defense; they argue that they are simply reporting information rather than distributing it for purposes of trade. This defense is extremely limited and is highly unlikely to protect a PR manager. For example, a court that might allow a newspaper to print a story about an individual would be less likely to allow that publication to use the individual's likeness in an advertisement that promotes sales of the publication. Since public relations managers frequently use communications for purposes of trade, a court would be unlikely to allow them to use newsworthiness as a defense.

Distorted or Fictional Portrayals

Sometimes a photograph is a legitimate representation of a person, but becomes distorted when it is communicated in a different context. This context, called "false light," could occur if the photo is included with dissimilar images; with a caption that provides an incorrect interpretation of the image; or in a story totally unrelated to the situation in which the image was taken.

For example, if a photograph of a married couple kissing at their twenty-fifth anniversary party was used in an article about how irresponsible sexual behavior could lead to the transmission of the AIDS virus, the couple could sue for invasion of privacy through "false light."

False light is "the dissemination of highly offensive false publicity about someone with knowledge or reckless disregard for the falsity."[2] It is usually applied to photographs, but a "false-light" suit can be filed over printed material as well. The publication or broadcast violation can occur in any of the standard public relations forms, including press release, brochure, video news release, etc.

False-light suits are based on two actions: distortion and fictionalization.

Distortion, which is more common, usually involves the omission of information or the presentation of information in a context that leads the viewer to a false conclusion. Fictionalization occurs when a published or broadcast report includes fictional characters, dialogue, or thoughts that are reported as facts. The fictionalization does not have to be negative to be the subject of such a lawsuit—neutral, even flattering information can be considered a representation in false light as long as it is fiction.

Although false-light litigation relates to publicity, the defense is often similar to that of a libel suit. For example, the defense may argue that:

- The context for the presentation is essentially true.
- The image has not been widely disseminated.
- The people in the photograph are not adequately identified for the suit to have merit.
- The falsification was inconsequential or, conversely, was so outrageous that the normal reader would recognize that the information was fictional.

Protection of Private Facts

Protection of private or potentially embarrassing facts has become an area of intense interest in public relations during the last decade, in large part because of computers—far more personal information is stored in them and distributed through them than ever before.

The private-facts tort is publication of private information that "(a) would be highly offensive to a reasonable person and (b) is not of legitimate concern to the public."[3] Both of these conditions must be met, and the courts have set a relatively high standard for each.

Private-facts cases involving public relations practitioners frequently involve the practitioner as plaintiff rather than defendant.

Plaintiffs seldom win these suits; when they do, it is usually in cases brought because of the distribution of medical information.

The safest defense in privacy cases is consent; the best and most common defense is newsworthiness.

When public relations managers conduct interviews, they should explain at the outset the intended and possible uses of the information that may be elicited; when possible, managers should obtain written consent for the use of the information. The consent should cover as many uses as possible and state the duration of the

7.11: Watch Those "Where Are They Now?" Segments

To maintain a link with your organization's past, you decide to start a "Where Are They Now?" section in your publication. Since you'll be using archived material that was already published by your company or a newspaper, there shouldn't be any legal questions regarding privacy, right?

Technically, yes. In practice, however, you need to be careful.

A number of individuals have sued newspapers that have run such segments. They reason that the original information in the story is now outdated, and that rerunning that information is no longer newsworthy.

If you disagree with this reasoning, you aren't alone—the courts disagreed with it as well. But the organizations still had to spend a lot of time and money defending themselves. And these are media organizations—remember that the courts tend to give less protection in these areas to public relations organizations, who would arguably be distributing information for the purposes of trade.

The lesson? Even the most innocuous stories can occasionally lead to problems. Get a consent form signed by the subjects of the article—then you'll never have to worry about where they are.

consent. If reporters misrepresent themselves to public relations managers before interviews, or if managers misrepresent themselves to subjects to obtain information, neither can claim implied consent for the interview—both would be vulnerable to private-facts lawsuits should they publish potentially embarrassing information.

Unlike in libel cases, the truth is not recognized as a defense in a private facts suit. On the other hand, a libel plaintiff can win a case based on distribution of damaging information to just one person, but a private-facts plaintiff must prove the information was distributed to a larger audience. However, the audience may be limited if it consists of people having a "special relationship" with the plaintiff (*Miller v. Motorola, Inc.* [1990]).

In a newsworthiness defense, public relations managers argue that the information is of legitimate news interest and therefore appropriate for dissemination. They may also argue that the information has been published in official government records and is therefore already public information.

Intrusion and Trespassing

How far can the public relations practitioner go to collect information? And how far can the media go?

These questions are addressed in the area of privacy law called intrusion and trespass. Intrusion is "a highly intrusive physical, electronic or mechanical invasion of another's solitude or seclusion."[4] Trespass occurs when a person "enters private property without consent of the owner or 'possessor' of the property."[5] In either case, it is irrelevant what information is gathered or whether that information is eventually broadcast or printed—it is the act of intrusion or trespass that is the focal point of the crime.

The central question in an intrusion case is where the information is gathered: Is it collected in a public place where it is reasonable to expect individuals to consider that someone else might hear or see what they are doing? Or in a private place where it is reasonable for an individual to assume that what he or she is saying or doing is private and, therefore, protected?

This division may appear distinct, but the courts have had some problems applying the rule. Normally, public relations practitioners and the media are permitted to collect any information of public interest that can be gathered in a public place. Public restau-

7.12: Telephone Tapes

Should you tape a telephone conversation with a reporter? Can that reporter tape you?

Both of you may want to tape the conversation to keep a record of what is said. PR practitioners and reporters tape conversations to protect themselves and may decide not to inform the other party because it might reduce that person's candor in the conversation.

Is it legal? According to federal law, you don't have to inform the other party if you wish to tape the conversation. Although the Federal Communications Commission has ruled that telephone companies must prohibit subscribers from recording phone conversations unless everyone in the conversation knows it is being taped, this practice is rarely enforced. On the other hand, a dozen states have laws prohibiting participant tape recordings.

Legal issues aside, an ethical issue remains: Would you want your phone conversation taped without your knowledge?

You can clear up any ambiguity by obtaining consent. If you want to tape a telephone conversation, ask permission before the conversation begins. If permission is granted, begin the taping, state when the tape is being made, and identify who is included in the conversation. Then ask for permission to tape. If you want to back up the consent even more thoroughly, obtain a written agreement from each party before the conversation.

The tape recorder should emit a beep at least every fifteen seconds, indicating that the conversation is being taped. This tone should be set so that all parties can hear it clearly.

rants are public places; private restaurants are not. Courtrooms that allow photography are public places, homes are not. On rare occasions an individual is so famous and press coverage so overzealous that courts have attempted to curtail media aggression by identifying a specific zone of privacy for a person, even in public places. For example, photographer Ron Gallela was ordered not to take pictures of Jacqueline Kennedy Onassis from closer than 150 feet. He appealed the ruling, and a federal court reduced the distance to 25 feet.

Physical space is only one protected area, however. Communications systems are another. It is an invasion of privacy for a journalist or public relations practitioner to tap telephone lines; intercept cell or microwave phone transmissions, video teleconferences or satellite transmissions; open mail; or access computer files, E-mails, phone messages, or previously recorded conversations to which they were not a party.

Law enforcement authorities may do these things, but only after obtaining a search warrant related to a specific crime.

Trespass can occur on physical property or on the Internet. Internet trespass cases have increased as advertisers have used specific Web sites or networks to "spam," or send out unsolicited messages in bulk form.

The courts have ruled that journalists who enter business establishments as regular customers have the right to do so, but journalists who misrepresent themselves to gain access (for example, by lying on employment applications) are guilty of trespassing.

If a person trespasses to obtain information and provides that information to the media, the media may print or broadcast it without fear of prosecution for the trespass. However, prosecutors may consider another charge: receiving stolen goods.

Conclusion

The public relations manager should be as familiar as possible with communications law for a number of reasons. Knowing the law helps managers clarify their rights and responsibilities and establish a more equitable relationship with lawyers when legal and public relations solutions are needed. More important, however, is that a working knowledge of communications law can help prevent entanglements that drain time and financial resources. Working within the parameters of the law will allow managers to concentrate on what they do best: practice public relations.

Action Plan

1. Arrange a meeting with your organization's chief legal adviser. Explain the benefits of public relations from a legal perspective, and ask for input on how the legal and public relations departments can best work together during situations that call for advice from both groups.
2. Read and keep on hand a primer devoted to communications law.
3. Before a legal situation can occur, meet with senior management to explain how public relations actions work with legal actions to protect the interests of the organization.

Exercises
No. 1: From Today's Headlines ...

Every day, newspapers carry stories about organizations addressing issues with legal and public relations ramifications. Select some as springboards for discussion with your staff and legal department to see how your organization would handle the situations.

No. 2: Overcoming the Barrister's Barriers

As this chapter points out, when CEOs get conflicting advice from legal counsel and public relations counsel, most tend to go with the legal advice. Develop a multi-point argument *against* that decision. Point out how legal strategies can have negative long-term implications and how public relations strategies can have positive short- and long-term implications. Present your position to the top levels of your organization *before* the next legal/public relations conflict occurs.

No. 3: The Court and the Court of Public Opinion

Identify the differences and similarities in tactics, audiences, and objectives between legal and public relations functions. Determine the points at which legal and public relations positions differ and the points at which they are the same. Understanding these similarities and differences will help you make the strongest possible argument for public relations decisions during future situations that involve the legal department.

CHAPTER 8

Ethics

The more influential any individual or profession is,
the greater the need for ethics.
—Philip Seib and Kathy Fitzpatrick

Sooner or later, everyone sits down to
a banquet of consequences.
—Robert Louis Stevenson

T
o the cynic, the term "public relations ethics" is an oxy-
moron. Attacks on the professionals range from statements such as "All they do is lie," to disparaging labels like
"spin doctor" and "flack."

It doesn't have to be that way. When public relations activities
are conducted professionally and ethically, they contribute to both
clients and society. As practitioners move into the ranks of management, they frequently recognize that ethical conduct is not just the
right thing to do—it makes good business sense as well.

That's because, at its core, public relations is about credibility.
And when practitioners take shortcuts, they sacrifice that often-irre-
trievable commodity.

In the short term, practitioners can agree with clients they
know are wrong, lie to reporters and get away with it, maybe even get
creative with their billable hours. But the long-term loss will always be

bigger than the short-term gain. This is a relationship-building business, and nothing is more damaging to a relationship than a lack of
trust. When you take ethical shortcuts, you take risks with your credibility. When practitioners lose their credibility, they are no longer
effective in the public relations business.

"The definitive reward for the unprincipled, profit-driven practitioner may be loss of credibility, clients and clout,"[1] warn Seib and
Fitzpatrick.

Public relations managers are tempted to take ethical shortcuts
on a regular basis. The most successful ones recognize that profits
don't come at the expense of ethics and that, in fact, the two go hand
in hand.

This chapter discusses the reasons the field of public relations
is perceived as unethical; reviews managers' relationships with various audiences; identifies the main areas of potential ethical dilem-
mas; and concludes with the PRSA Code of Ethics, a set of guidelines that can help clarify the managers' professional standards and
practices.

Why Is PR Considered Unethical?

There are a number of reasons that public relations has a reputation
for unethical conduct. Unfortunately, the first is that the allegation is
sometimes true—some people in the profession do not operate
truthfully and ethically. Lying, dissembling, profiting from undisclosed relationships, and similar actions reinforce the perception of
public relations as a devious profession. When such unsavory activities end up in public view, they get a lot of exposure. While most professionals who conduct themselves in an unethical manner end up
hurting themselves by losing credibility, they also harm the profession as a whole.

In many cases, unethical conduct comes from people who are
not even public relations professionals. This leads to the second reason
for a tarnished reputation. Other professions have established screening processes (national examinations, certifications, etc.), but anyone

may claim membership in the public relations field. While this inclusiveness offers some advantages, one unfortunate result is clear: a lot of unqualified, unethical people *claim* to be working in public relations.

For decades, dedicated professionals have attempted to develop more formal, rigorous approaches to entering the profession. There have been significant improvements, such as accreditation programs, but these efforts do not prevent people with neither background nor training in public relations from calling themselves practitioners. While accreditation and certification do not eliminate unethical conduct, it is clear that some form of professional training can at least help practitioners to identify and address ethical issues.

Further fueling the negative perception is a misunderstanding of the relationships between practitioners and the people with whom they work. In sales, purchasing, and many other areas of business, professional relationships are clear—and so are the rules governing them.

The public relations manager, on the other hand, interacts with a variety of people and organizations under changing, nuanced, and unstated rules. A manager may be dealing with agency executives, employees, clients, and the media. These roles and responsibilities differ and are often misunderstood—sometimes by the participants and frequently by the general public. Seib and Fitzpatrick note:

> Opinions about public relations are often affected by lack of clarity about just who true public relations professionals are. Even journalists, who have frequent, direct contact with public relations practitioners, sometimes are uninformed or misinformed about the true nature of public relations work.[2]

Another source of misunderstanding is the nature of public relations services. The intangibility of the end product may produce confusion and suspicion—even among clients.

Finally, there is the frequent blurring of the messenger, the message, and the source. Many times, the best a public relations manager can do is help an organization deliver bad news. However, when practitioners represent that organization, they may also be stained by the information they are disseminating—even when they had nothing to do with it. Unfortunately, "much of the distrust of public relations professionals derives from the lack of public trust in the institutions they represent,"[3] Seib and Fitzpatrick note.

The profession faces a permanent, uphill battle to maintain ethical standards and educate a dubious public about the value of public relations activity. Some credibility issues are beyond the manager's control; many are not. When managers strive to familiarize themselves with the profession's ethical standards and work to integrate these standards into their organization's day-to-day actions, they help the profession improve and gain acceptance.

Clarifying the Roles

Because so many relationships may influence managers' conduct, ethical behavior begins by clarifying each role in the process. "To whom is moral duty owed?" ask Christians et al. in their book *Media Ethics: Cases and Moral Reasoning.*

> Many times, in the consideration of ethics, direct conflicts arise between the rights of one person or group and those of others. Policies and actions inevitably must favor some to the exclusion of others. Often our most agonizing dilemmas revolve around our primary obligation to a person or a group. Or we ask ourselves, is my first loyalty to my company or to a particular client?[4]

The authors identify five categories of obligation:

1. Duty to oneself
2. Duty to clients/subscribers/supporters
3. Duty to our organization or firm
4. Duty to professional colleagues
5. Duty to society

By clarifying and prioritizing these categories for themselves, managers can help guide the business practices of their organizations in many ways, from day-to-day decisions to long-term policies. Through their words and actions, managers set the spirit—often the letter—of ethical rules for lower-level employees. Their ethics reverberate throughout the organization.

Danger Zones

Ethical practices will be tested most frequently in three areas: soliciting business, conflict of interest, and media relations.

Soliciting Business

The initial contact with a potential client forms the basis for any subsequent relationship. There are three primary ethical considerations in solicitation: representing unethical clients, respecting current relationships, and guaranteeing the outcome of services.

CONTROVERSIAL CLIENTS

The manager should begin by considering the ethical positions of potential clients. Some practitioners argue that the public relations profession should mirror the legal profession, and that everyone who wants representation should be able to get it. But legal representation is guaranteed by the Constitution; public relations representation is not.

The decision to represent a controversial or unpopular client is both an ethical and a business decision. Will existing or potential clients decline managers' services because they took on particular clients? Will the managers' relationships with the media or other members of the profession be diminished? Obviously, it is difficult for managers to limit themselves to clients with whom they agree on all issues, but they should still weigh the impact of new clients on their organization's image and other ramifications of the decision before taking on a controversial client.

Infringing on client relationships is a gray area. It would be difficult to expand your business if you sought only clients without representation. Nevertheless, it is unethical to deliberately communicate misinformation or negative information about a competitor to obtain a contract.

When soliciting business, managers should refrain from guaranteeing outcomes that are beyond their control. Managers may ethically guarantee clients that they will develop materials and work with editors to maximize the chances for client exposure in various venues, but it is not ethical to guarantee placement in a specific publication.

Contingency fees reflect the blurred ethical boundaries of performance guarantees. The PRSA Code of Ethics does not ban these arrangements, but many practitioners frown on them because they (1) consider the arrangement a guarantee, (2) recognize that its fulfillment involves factors beyond their control, and (3) fear damage to clients' long-term relationships if the results fall short.

Conflict of Interest

As practitioners change jobs more often, agencies and industries grow and merge, and clients expand their products and services, the potential for conflicts of interest increases dramatically. The manager should consider both perceived and real conflicts, and internal (in-house) conflicts as well as external ones with clients, other agencies, and the media. Most conflicts of interest can be addressed through a simple policy: full disclosure. When an agency commits to disclosing all relationships to clients, potential clients, members of the media, and interested publics, the potential for conflicts of interest is sharply curtailed.

Full disclosure does not *eliminate* conflicts or accusations of conflicts, but it gives all parties enough information to weigh the ethical implications of relationships, minimize misunderstanding and suspicion, and provide a strong defense if allegations arise.

Media Relations

While this area includes a multitude of ethical considerations, one maxim applies at all times: don't lie to the press.

"A lie is a lie is a lie," state Howard and Mathews in their book, *On Deadline: Managing Media Relations.*

> No good comes of lying; particularly from lying to the media. A lie will come out in print or on television. It will be taken as truth by the public who, when they later discover the real story will disbelieve anything further that the organization says.

The authors add:

> Lying in public is no different from lying in the courtroom under oath. The sentence, however, can be tougher: loss of credibility, loss of respect, loss of customers, loss of trust by the community, and by shareholders. There is no such thing as a "half-lie," a "small lie" or a "white lie." The adjective does not detract from the noun, rather, the adjective enhances it.[5]

The same holds true for half-truths and selective disclosures that may be accurate but misleading, or information the manager believed to be true but later turned out to be false. The bottom line is this: A manager has an ethical obligation to communicate in a way that does not mislead members of the press or public.

Other ethical concerns should attend your ongoing press relations. The press/public relations relationship is a complex one—neither wholly cooperative nor wholly adversarial. Public relations managers will be most effective if they take time to understand the journalist's mission. Conflicts may be subtle.

8.1: Quote-Making

The Ethics of Quote-Making
by Michael J. Bugeja

Every day, public relations practitioners send out news releases that include, for a lack of a better word, "invented" quotations.

These "invented" quotes are phrases or ideas that a client never actually says verbatim, but are nonetheless attributed to him or her inside quotation marks. Often, these quotes have been based on notes or conversations with the client. However, in the strictest sense, the words usually are a composite of real and made-up statements.

Hence the term "quote-making."

There are legal and ethical risks to manufacturing quotes for mass distribution. Because contents of news releases may appear in mass media, quote-making can be called into question, given the right set of circumstances.

Despite the widespread practice, most practitioners are reluctant to discuss the subject. In the book, *The Practice of Public Relations,* Fraser P. Seitel writes:

> Like it or not, public relations people do indeed fabricate statements for their employers. It goes with the territory. And if such statements are approved by employers in advance, ethical questions are less pertinent. However, PR people rarely announce or even acknowledge that they have authored such statements.

Of course, a lot would have to go wrong for a PR quote-making case to make legal history. The PR writer would have to invent a quote that was not reviewed or pre-approved by the client, was released to the media, and contained a quotation that somehow resulted in the client's loss of business or damage to his or her reputation.

Those might seem like acceptable risks to an experienced practitioner. Rarely are news releases sent out with client approval.

And when they do, the decision usually involves a deadline or other time constraint.

High Risk

However, the risk of something going awry remains, especially if younger, less-experienced practitioners are involved. An account executive, for example, could very easily misinterpret a client's words or invent a quote that's not 100 percent accurate or is a flat-out lie.

A case study in the Fall 1994 issue of Public Relations Review illustrates the point. In *Lies, Deceptions, and Public Relations*, the authors, Elaine E. Englehardt and DeAnn Evans, discuss a quote invented by a hospital's house organ writer. The writer heralded the hospital's "charitable care account" in a quote claiming that the hospital picked up the $130,004.99 tab for a patient who delivered a premature baby. Not true, according to the patient (who was also a reporter), who claims her insurance company and not the charity account paid the bill.

Englehardt and Evans wrote:

> The writer for the house organ lied. The emotional story needed something to compel readers to donate, so a quote was added. It was a lie, one that hurt the parents, the hospital, the reputation of the house organ, and perhaps the charitable arm of the hospital.

Practitioners Debate Practice

Not all practitioners condone quote-making, even with a client's pre-approval. Dan Pinger, APR, Fellow PRSA, president of Dan Pinger Public Relations in Cincinnati, says PR writers should quote sources verbatim. "A major concern in PR is credibility, and that comes from authenticity," he says. "A communication that is other than the real spoken word might not ring true." Practitioners at his agency, he adds, "sit face-to-face with a person to be quoted and take accurate notes. It's different if we are working on a statement; then we work together."

John Paluszek, president of Ketchum Public Affairs, is not a fan of manufactured quotes either. "It would boggle my mind that any PR person would create a statement (not based on notes) that really isn't representative of the client's views and then release it. One misrepresentation is about all that would be tolerated."

Indeed. Paluszek points out that Larry Speakes, former press secretary to President Reagan and Merrill Lynch communications executive, probably "lost his job over this exact issue." In his 1988 book *Speaking Out,* Speakes disclosed that he fabricated statements and attributed them to Reagan at a Geneva conference without the President's approval. At the time, the disclosure conflicted with Merrill's "Tradition of Trust" campaign, and Speakes resigned soon after.

The anecdote is pertinent today. Values and mission statements are becoming increasingly popular at PR agencies. Such documents can ensure sound business practices, enhance corporate philosophy, and serve as a guide during crises.

In unforeseen circumstances, however, the practice of drafting quotes without client approval may be necessary and defensible. Says Jim Little, president of First Communications in Findlay, Ohio:

> If you are working with somebody and have a close, personal relationship and know what he or she thinks then quote-making can be a standard practice. The most preferable way would be to interview the person, but on a practical day-to-day basis that first step sometimes gets omitted.

Although PR executives may differ on the ethics of quote-making, all emphasize these ethical components: intimate knowledge of a client and an account; accurate note-taking during sessions with clients; client review and pre-approval of direct quotations.

Is Pre-Approval Enough?

Review and pre-approval from a client is the pivotal ethical component. "The process allows credibility" says John Berard. "You ask, 'What do you think?' You get to know the client's view and bring your experience to bear. You play back the quote to the

Paying a reporter to write a story is unethical, but what about "rewarding" an influential reporter who has written a positive story by providing an exclusive? How about picking up the tab for a lunch meeting or holiday gifts for the manager's regular press contacts? These questions are more subjective, and may depend on the standards and policy of each party. Many news organizations explicitly forbid such gifts and favors.

As a general rule, the manager should avoid situations that appear to obligate a reporter. When in doubt, opt out.

Conclusions

Most public relations managers conduct their business ethically, professionally, and responsibly. The complexity and the number of roles demand that managers understand and follow the rules of each. When managers articulate and practice an ethical approach to their duties, they will have a positive effect on their organizations' cultures—and ultimately on the profession as a whole.

8.2: PRSA Code of Ethics and Ethics Pledge—2000

The Public Relations Society of America (PRSA) is America's leading organization in promoting and maintaining professional standards of the profession. The society has a long history of standards development, and in 2000 it released the following revised code of ethics:

PREAMBLE

PUBLIC RELATIONS SOCIETY OF AMERICA MEMBER CODE OF ETHICS 2000

Professional Values
Principles of Conduct
Commitment and Compliance

This Code applies to PRSA members. The Code is designed to be a useful guide for PRSA members as they carry out their ethical responsibilities. This document is designed to anticipate and accommodate, by precedent, ethical challenges that may arise. The scenarios outlined in the Code provision are actual examples of misconduct. More will be added as experience with the Code occurs.

The Public Relations Society of America (PRSA) is committed to ethical practices. The level of public trust PRSA members seek, as we serve the public good, means we have taken on a special obligation to operate ethically.

The value of member reputation depends upon the ethical conduct of everyone affiliated with the Public Relations Society of America. Each of us sets an example for each other—as well as other professionals—by our pursuit of excellence with powerful standards of performance, professionalism, and ethical conduct.

Emphasis on enforcement of the Code has been eliminated. But, the PRSA Board of Directors retains the right to bar from membership or expel from the Society any individual who has been or is sanctioned by a government agency or convicted in a court of law of an action that is in violation of this Code.

Ethical practice is the most important obligation of a PRSA member. We view the Member Code of Ethics as a model for other professions, organizations, and professionals.

PRSA MEMBER STATEMENT OF PROFESSIONAL VALUES

This statement presents the core values of PRSA members and, more broadly, of the public relations profession. These values provide the foundation for the Member Code of Ethics and set the industry standard for the professional practice of public relations. These values are the fundamental beliefs that guide our behaviors and decision-making process. We believe our professional values are vital to the integrity of the profession as a whole.

Advocacy
We serve the public interest by acting as responsible advocates for those we represent. We provide a voice in the marketplace of ideas, facts, and viewpoints to aid informed public debate.

Honesty
We adhere to the highest standards of accuracy and truth in advancing the interests of those we represent and in communicating with the public.

Expertise
We acquire and responsibly use specialized knowledge and experience.
We advance the profession through continued professional development, research, and education.
We build mutual understanding, credibility, and relationships among a wide array of institutions and audiences.

INDEPENDENCE

We provide objective counsel to those we represent.
We are accountable for our actions.

Loyalty
We are faithful to those we represent, while honoring our obligation
to serve the public interest.

Fairness
We deal fairly with clients, employers, competitors, peers, vendors,
the media, and the general public.
We respect all opinions and support the right of free expression.

PRSA CODE PROVISIONS

Free Flow Of Information

Core Principle
Protecting and advancing the free flow of accurate and truthful
information is essential to serving the public interest and contribut-
ing to informed decision making in a democratic society.

Intent
To maintain the integrity of relationships with the media, govern-
ment officials, and the public.
To aid informed decision-making.

Guidelines
A member shall:
Preserve the integrity of the process of communication.
Be honest and accurate in all communications.
Act promptly to correct erroneous communications for which the
practitioner is responsible.
Preserve the free flow of unprejudiced information when giving or
receiving gifts by ensuring that gifts are nominal, legal, and
infrequent.

EXAMPLES OF IMPROPER CONDUCT UNDER THIS PROVISION:

A member representing a ski manufacturer gives a pair of expensive racing skis to a sports magazine columnist, to influence the columnist to write favorable articles about the product.

A member entertains a government official beyond legal limits and/or in violation of government reporting requirements.

COMPETITION

Core Principle
Promoting healthy and fair competition among professionals preserves an ethical climate while fostering a robust business environment.

Intent
To promote respect and fair competition among public relations professionals.

To serve the public interest by providing the widest choice of practitioner options.

Guidelines
A member shall:

Follow ethical hiring practices designed to respect free and open competition without deliberately undermining a competitor.

Preserve intellectual property rights in the marketplace.

Examples of Improper Conduct Under This Provision
A member employed by a "client organization" shares helpful information with a counseling firm that is competing with others for the organization's business.

A member spreads malicious and unfounded rumors about a competitor in order to alienate the competitor's clients and employees in a ploy to recruit people and business.

DISCLOSURE OF INFORMATION

Core Principle

Open communication fosters informed decision making in a democratic society.

Intent

To build trust with the public by revealing all information needed for responsible decision making.

Guidelines

A member shall:

Be honest and accurate in all communications.

Act promptly to correct erroneous communications for which the member is responsible.

Investigate the truthfulness and accuracy of information released on behalf of those represented.

Reveal the sponsors for causes and interests represented.

Disclose financial interest (such as stock ownership) in a client's organization.

Avoid deceptive practices.

Examples of Improper Conduct Under this Provision:

Front groups: A member implements "grass roots" campaigns or letter-writing campaigns to legislators on behalf of undisclosed interest groups.

Lying by omission: A practitioner for a corporation knowingly fails to release financial information, giving a misleading impression of the corporation's performance.

A member discovers inaccurate information disseminated via a Web site or media kit and does not correct the information.

A member deceives the public by employing people to pose as volunteers to speak at public hearings and participate in "grass roots" campaigns.

SAFEGUARDING CONFIDENCES

Core Principle

Client trust requires appropriate protection of confidential and private information.

Intent

To protect the privacy rights of clients, organizations, and individuals by safeguarding confidential information.

Guidelines

A member shall:

Safeguard the confidences and privacy rights of present, former, and prospective clients and employees.

Protect privileged, confidential, or insider information gained from a client or organization.

Immediately advise an appropriate authority if a member discovers that confidential information is being divulged by an employee of a client company or organization.

Examples of Improper Conduct Under This Provision

A member changes jobs, takes confidential information, and uses that information in the new position to the detriment of the former employer.

A member intentionally leaks proprietary information to the detriment of some other party.

CONFLICTS OF INTEREST

Core Principle

Avoiding real, potential, or perceived conflicts of interest builds the trust of clients, employers, and the publics.

Intent

To earn trust and mutual respect with clients or employers.

To build trust with the public by avoiding or ending situations that put one's personal or professional interests in conflict with society's interests.

Guidelines

A member shall:

Act in the best interests of the client or employer, even subordinating the member's personal interests.

Avoid actions and circumstances that may appear to compromise good business judgment or create a conflict between personal and professional interests.

Disclose promptly any existing or potential conflict of interest to affected clients or organizations.

Encourage clients and customers to determine if a conflict exists after notifying all affected parties.

Examples of Improper Conduct Under This Provision

The member fails to disclose that he or she has a strong financial interest in a client's chief competitor.

The member represents a "competitor company" or a "conflicting interest" without informing a prospective client.

ENHANCING THE PROFESSION

Core Principle

Public relations professionals work constantly to strengthen the public's trust in the profession.

Intent

To build respect and credibility with the public for the profession of public relations.

To improve, adapt, and expand professional practices.

Guidelines

A member shall:

Acknowledge that there is an obligation to protect and enhance the profession.

Keep informed and educated about practices in the profession to ensure ethical conduct.

Actively pursue personal professional development.

Decline representation of clients or organizations that urge or require actions contrary to this Code.

Accurately define what public relations activities can accomplish.

Counsel subordinates in proper ethical decision making.

Require that subordinates adhere to the ethical requirements of the Code.

Report ethical violations, whether committed by PRSA members or not, to the appropriate authority.

Examples of Improper Conduct Under This Provision

A PRSA member declares publicly that a product the client sells is safe, without disclosing evidence to the contrary.

A member initially assigns some questionable client work to a non-member practitioner to avoid the ethical obligation of PRSA membership.

PRSA Member Code of Ethics Pledge

I pledge:

To conduct myself professionally, with truth, accuracy, fairness, and responsibility to the public; To improve my individual competence and advance the knowledge and proficiency of the profession through continuing research and education; And to adhere to the articles of the Member Code of Ethics 2000 for the practice of public relations as adopted by the governing Assembly of the Public Relations Society of America.

I understand and accept that there is a consequence for misconduct, up to and including membership revocation.

And, I understand that those who have been or are sanctioned by a government agency or convicted in a court of law of an action that is in violation of this Code may be barred from membership or expelled from the Society.[*]

*Excerpted from PRSA Code of Ethics—2000 <hwww.prsa.org/codeofethics.html>.

Copyright 2000 by *Public Relations Tactics*. Reprinted with permission from PRSA.

Action Plan

It is just as important to develop and maintain your ethical code as it is to develop your skill sets in other areas.

1. If your organization has a code of ethics, familiarize yourself with it. The code often reflects the ethical perspectives of the organization's leaders, and it is useful to understand where they are coming from.
2. If your organization does *not* have a code of ethics, work with fellow employees to draft one and submit it to the president of your organization for review. This will give everyone an opportunity to refocus their efforts in this area, and can lead to some productive discussions about the ethical principles that guide your organization.
3. Write your own ethical code for the public relations business. You can use the PRSA Code of Ethics as a model.
4. When dealing with clients, regularly refer to ethics to ensure that they understand your position. Telegraphing your position early can save you from facing unethical proposals in the future. It will also enhance your reputation.

Exercises

No. 1: Ethics Up Front

Develop a set of ethical questions for potential employees. The best time to deal with ethical issues is during the interview, to determine whether a candidate shares your code. Make ethics an important component of each hiring decision.

No. 2: On-the-Job Training

Many younger practitioners have neither experience nor history with professional ethics, so good managers include these issues in general business discussions. Develop a set of scenarios to test ethical issues; introduce these scenarios into discussions with members of the staff, during and after work, to monitor their ethical development.

No. 3: Managing Media Relations

One of the most ambiguous areas of ethics is media relations. Develop a concrete set of dos and don'ts for your employees, so that their interaction with members of the press is clear, effective, and above board. Members of the press also make ethical mistakes, so your employees should also have a thorough understanding of journalistic rules of conduct.

CHAPTER 9

Conclusions

There's no feeling quite like the one you get when you get to the truth: You're the captain of the ship called you. You're setting the course, the speed, and you're out there on the bridge, steering.
—Carl Frederick

This book is just one tool in your ongoing development as a public relations manager. You can use it to familiarize yourself with some of the techniques and strategies practitioners use to advance to higher-level roles within their organizations.

Now, consider how you can develop additional management tools in each key area covered in this text. In client and personnel relations, for example, examine not only the current state of your relationships with these critical people, but also determine where you want these relationships to go, how you can help get them there, and how you can forge new relationships.

Research and finance are two areas where public relations practitioners are often weakest. If these are uncomfortable topics for you, recognize these obstacles and challenge yourself to address them. Closing these gaps in your skill base can be one of the quickest roads to advancement.

Crisis situations can be tremendous opportunities for you to contribute to an organization's development and thus gain the recognition of top management. Technological development in the public relations industry is inevitable. Master it, and you can use it to your advantage and provide exceptional service to your clients. Finally, legal and ethical knowledge can serve as the basis for your further development as a sound, reliable source of guidance in your organization. The people you want to work with are the ones who recognize the importance of these considerations.

Your development as a manager is a work in progress, and you will need to continually update and improve your management skills. Whether familiarizing yourself with the latest media relations software packages, developing your organization's business plan, or learning new motivation techniques for staff, you will always need to learn more about the role and methods of public relations management.

Fortunately, the profession continues to develop as well. Many

9.1: Web Sites to Boost Your Professional Development

If you are interested in learning more about public relations management, you may want to consult some relevant Internet sites. The sites listed below include information on career development, ethical issues, industry practices, and professional organizations.

The Public Relations Society of America (PRSA):
<http://www.prsa.org>
International Association of Business Communicators (IABC):
<www.iabc.com>
American Communication Association (ACA):
<www.americancomm.org>
The Institute for PR: <www.instituteforpr.com>
Association for Education in Journalism and Mass Communication
(AEJMC) Public Relations Division:
<http://lamar.colostate.edu/~aejmcpr>
The Center for Public Integrity:
<www.publicintegrity.org/main.html>

seasoned PR professionals are available to help guide your development, through professional organizations; career development seminars and conferences; research and professional literature and Web
sites that can help keep you current on topics in the business.

"A wise man learns from his mistakes," so the proverb goes, "but
a wiser man learns from the mistakes of others." If you take advantage
of the experience of seasoned managers and continue to develop
your skills in key areas, you will help bring the public relations profession to that coveted place in an organization—a seat at the management table.

As you work to improve your skills and advance in your career,
keep in mind that increased stature comes with increased responsi-

---

American Society of Association Executives (ASAE):
    <www.asaenet.org>
National Investor Relations Institute: <www.niri.org>
The Museum of Public Relations: <www.prmuseum.com>
PR Week: <www.prweekus.com>
PR News: <www.prandmarketing.com/cgi/catalog/
    info?PRN>
O'Dwyer's: <www.odwyerpr.com>
Silver Anvil Resource Center: <www.silveranvil.org>

    At this writing, three additional sites are designed to provide
up-to-date information on on-line resources:

On-line Public Relations: <www.online-pr.com>
Public Relations Links: <http://lamar.colostate.edu/
    ~hallahan/j13pr.htm>
PRPlace: <www.prplace.com>

---

bility. The best managers take an interest in the professional development of their staffs as well. This investment has tangible rewards, of course: you are able to delegate more work, therefore freeing you to spend more time on management functions. But there are also important intangible results: you will receive the satisfaction that comes with helping shape the careers of those who succeed you and making a truly significant contribution to your profession.

Bring the same creativity and passion to your career improvement that you bring to your client services, and, ultimately, do what you would like your clients to do—give yourself credit when you make progress!

Action Plan

This book has introduced you to the key concepts you must address to move into a management role in public relations. The final action plan is to use this information to transform yourself into a manager.

1. Write each chapter area at the top of a blank page (client relations, personnel, research, crisis communications, finance, new technology, legal considerations, and ethics), divide the page into two columns, and then list your strengths and weaknesses in each area.
2. Assign an overall grade to yourself for each area, then rank the areas to identify your greatest strengths and weaknesses.
3. For each area, list specific activities you can do to increase your strengths and reduce your weaknesses. Note any significant deficiencies, set objectives for improving these areas, and use benchmarks to measure your progress.

Notes

Chapter 1

1. Ehling, William P., "Estimating the Value of Public Relations and Communication to an Organization," in *Excellence in Public Relations and Communication Management*, ed. Grunig, 619.
2. Nager, Norman R. and Richard H. Truitt, *Strategic Public Relations Counseling: Models from the Academy*, 140.
3. Broom, Glen M. and George D. Smith, "Testing the Practitioner's Impact on Clients," *Precision Public Relations*, ed. Hiebert, 312–14.
4. Ibid., 313.
5. Ibid., 314.
6. Ibid., 315.
7. Ibid., 313.
8. Howard, Carole M., "Skills You Need To Expand Your Counselor Role," *Public Relations Tactics*, October, 2000.
9. Dozier, David M., Larissa A. Grunig, and James E. Grunig, *Manager's Guide to Excellence in Public Relations and Communication Management*, 76.
10. Howard.

Chapter 2

1. Cantor, Bill, *Inside Public Relations*, ed. Burger (Longman, Inc., 1989), 281.
2. Phipps, Kathy, "How I Became a Boss," *Public Relations Tactics*, August 1999.

3. Long, Janet Reswick, "How to Win the Hiring Game," Public Relations Society of America Web Site <http://www.prsa.org/c029822a.html>.
4. Ibid.
5. Ibid.
6. Bisbee, Jennifer, "The Survey Says—Outsourcing of PR Activities On the Rise," *Public Relations Tactics,* February 1998.
7. Howard, Carole M., "Outsourcing Turns Competitors Into Vital Partners," *Public Relations Tactics,* April 1996.
8. Bisbee, Jennifer, "Wish You Could Clone Yourself? All About Outsourcing," *Public Relations Tactics,* February 1998.
9. Paine, David, "It's Time to Put People Before Profit," *Public Relations Tactics,* December 1996.
10. Ibid.
11. FitzGerald, Suzanne Sparks, "Writing More Effectively on the Job," *Public Relations Tactics,* April 1999.
12. PRSA Web Site, accreditation section <www.accreditationboard.org>.

Chapter 3

1. Cutlip, Scott M., Allen H. Center, and Glen M. Broom, *Effective Public Relations* (Upper Saddle River, NJ: Prentice Hall, 2000), 343.
2. Ibid.

Chapter 4

1. Guth, David W., and Charles Marsh, *Public Relations: A Values-Driven Approach* (Needham Heights, MA: Allyn & Bacon, 2000), 394.
2. Ibid., 393.
3. Ibid., 394.
4. Wenger, Ty, "When the Sports Hits the Fan: Crisis PR in the Age of Athlete Scandals," *Public Relations Tactics,* March 1997.
5. Guth and Marsh, 388.
6. Henry, Rene A., *You'd Better Have a Hose if You Want to Put Out the Fire* (Windsor, CA: Gollywobbler Productions, 2000), 252.
7. Center, Allen, and Patrick Jackson, *Public Relations Practices: Managerial Case Studies and Problems* (Upper Saddle River, NJ: Prentice Hall, 1995), 423.
8. Henry, 254.

Chapter 5

1. Hendrix, Jerry A., *Public Relations Cases*, (Belmont, CA: Wadsworth Publishing, 1995), 259.

Chapter 6

1. Thomsen, Steven R., "Using Online Databases in Corporate Issues Management," *Public Relations Review* 21, no. 2, (1995), 110.
2. Petrison, Lisa A., and Paul Wang, "From Relationships to Relationship Marketing: Applying Database Technology to Public Relations," *Public Relations Review*, 19, no. 3, (1993), 237.
3. Ibid., 242.
4. Witmer, Diane F., *Spinning the Web: A Handbook for Public Relations on the Internet* (New York: Addison Wesley Longman, 2000), 95.
5. Ibid., 95.
6. Barks, Edward R., "To Web or Not to Web? That is the Question for Independent Practitioners," *Public Relations Tactics*, August 1999.
7. Witmer, Diane F., *Spinning the Web: A Handbook for Public Relations on the Internet* (New York: Addison Wesley Longman, 2000), 116.
8. Ibid., 118.
9. Newman, Kelli, "The Competitive Edge of Web Site Video—Are You Ready?" *Public Relations Tactics*, June 2000.
10. Content vs. Web Master: Tips and Techniques, PRSA Professional Resource Center
11. Witmer, 119.
12. Ibid., 103.
13. Excerpted from Harrison, Tony, "High-Tech, but Off-line—The CD-ROM," *Public Relations Tactics*, September 1996.

Chapter 7

1. Article 10, PRSA Code of Professional Standards for the Practice of Public Relations.
2. Restatement (Second) of Torts, sec 632E, (1977).
3. Ibid., sec. 652D, (1977).
4. Ibid., sec. 652B, (1977).
5. Ibid., sec 158 at 277 (1965).

Chapter 8

1. Seib, Philip, and Kathy Fitzpatrick, *Public Relations Ethics* (Orlando, FL: Harcourt Brace and Company, 1995), 39.
2. Ibid., 4.
3. Ibid., 7.
4. Christians, Clifford G. et. al, *Media Ethics: Cases and Moral Reasoning* (New York: Addison Wesley Longman, 2001), 21.
5. Howard, Carol and Wilma Mathews, *On Deadline: Managing Media Relations* (Prospect Heights, IL: Waveland Press, 1985), 98.

Bibliography

Abelsson, Mark. (1999). "Creating a More Inclusive Work Environment for Gay Men and Lesbians," *Public Relations Tactics*, March.

Anderson, Christian. (1999). "Financial PR: Opportunities by the Numbers," *Public Relations Tactics*, July.

Anderson, Curt. (1997). "Using an Intranet During a Crisis," *Public Relations Tactics,* May.

Austin, Erica Weintraub, and Bruce E. Pinkleton. (2001). *Strategic Public Relations Management: Planning and Managing Effective Communication Programs* (Mahwah, NJ: Lawrence Erlbaum Associates, Publishers).

Baker, Lee W. (1993). *The Credibility Factor: Putting Ethics to Work in Public Relations* (Homewood, Ill: Richard D. Irwin, Inc.).

Barks, Edward R. (1999) "To Web or Not to Web? That Is the Question for Independent Practitioners," *Public Relations Tactics,* August.

Bisbee, Jennifer. (1998). "The Survey Says—Outsourcing of PR Activities On the Rise," *Public Relations Tactics,* February.

_____. (1998). "Wish You Could Clone Yourself? All About Outsourcing," *Public Relations Tactics,* February.

Broom, Glen M., and George D. Smith. (1988). "Testing the Practitioner's Impact on Clients," *Precision Public Relations,* ed. Hiebert. (White Plains, NY: Longman, Inc.).

Bugeja, Michael J. (1996). "The Ethics of Quote-Making," *Public Relations Tactics,* September.

Cantor, Bill, (1989). *Experts in Action: Inside Public Relations* (White Plains, NY: Longman, Inc.).

_____. (1989). *Inside Public Relations,* ed., Burger (White Plains, NY: Longman, Inc.).

_____. (1983). "Winning Personality Traits: Ten Characteristics that Indicate Whether an Individual Will Be Successful in Public Relations," *Public Relations Journal,* June.

Caywood, Clarke L., ed. (1997). *The Handbook of Strategic Public Relations and Integrated Communications* (New York, NY: McGraw-Hill).

Center, Allen, and Patrick Jackson. (1995). *Public Relations Practices: Managerial Case Studies and Problems* (Upper Saddle River, NJ: Prentice Hall).

Christians, Clifford G., et. al. (2001). *Media Ethics: Cases and Moral Reasoning* (New York: Addison Wesley Longman).

Content vs. Web Master: Tips and Techniques, PRSA Professional Resource Center. <www.prsa.org/_resources/resources/contentvswm.asp>.

"Credibility Gap: Who Is Believed in a Crisis?" *Public Relations Tactics*, August 1996.

Cutlip, Scott M., Allen H. Center, and Glen M. Broom, *Effective Public Relations* (Upper Saddle River, NJ: Prentice Hall, 2000).

Dobens, Christopher. (1999). "The Lost Art of Writing in Public Relations," *Public Relations Tactics*, April.

Dozier, David M., Larissa A. Grunig, and James E. Grunig. (1995). *Manager's Guide to Excellence in Public Relations and Communication Management* (Mahwah, NJ: Lawrence Erlbaum Associates, Inc.).

Elsasser, John. (2001) Interview with Kathleen Larey Lewton in *Public Relations Tactics*, January.

_____. (1998). "Lawyers are Learning the Art of Public Relations." *Public Relations Tactics*, June.

Farinelli, Jean. (1996). "Salesmanship Starts When the Client Says No." *Public Relations Tactics*, September.

_____. (1996). "Tips for Agency-Client Relations." *Public Relations Tactics*, September.

FitzGerald, Suzanne Sparks. (1999). "Writing More Effectively on the Job." *Public Relations Tactics*, April.

Gaschen, Dennis John. (2001). "Web Sites You Need to Know About." *Public Relations Tactics*, May.

Gertz v. Robert Welch, Inc. (1974). 418 U.S. 323.

Guth, David W., and Charles Marsh. (2000). *Public Relations: A Values-Driven Approach* (Needham Heights, MA: Allyn & Bacon).

Grunig, James E., and Todd Hunt. (1984). *Managing Public Relations* (New York: CBS College Publishing).

Grunig, James E., ed. (1992). *Excellence in Public Relations and Communications Management* (Hillsdale, NJ: Lawrence Erlbaum Associates, Inc).

Harrison, Tony. (1996). "High-Tech But Off-Line—The CD-ROM." *Public Relations Tactics*, September.

Heath, Robert L., ed. (2001). *Handbook of Public Relations* (Thousand Oaks, CA: Sage Publications, Inc.).

Hendrix, Jerry A. (1995). *Public Relations Cases* (Belmont, CA: Wadsworth Publishing).

Henry, Rene A. (2000). *You'd Better Have a Hose If You Want To Put Out The Fire* (Windsor, CA: Gollywobbler Productions).

Hiebert, Ray Eldon, ed. (1988). *Precision Public Relations* (White Plains, NY: Longman).

Howard, Carole M. (1996). "Outsourcing Turns Competitors Into Vital Partners." *Public Relations Tactics,* April.

_____. (2000). "Skills You Need To Expand Your Counselor Role." *Public Relations Tactics,* October.

Howard, Carole M., and Wilma K. Mathews. (1985). *On Deadline: Managing Media Relations, 3e* (Prospect Heights, IL: Waveland Press).

Long, Janet Reswick. (2002). "How to Win the Hiring Game." Public Relations Society of America Web site <www.prsa.org/c029822a.html>.

Long, Richard K. (2001). "Realistic Drills Enhance Survival in Crisis." *Public Relations Tactics,* January.

Middleton, Kent R., Robert Trager, and Bill F. Chamberlin. (2001). *The Law of Public Communication* (New York: Addison Wesley Longman, Inc.).

McElreath, Mark P. (1996). *Managing Systematic and Ethical Public Relations Campaigns* (Madison, WI: Brown & Benchmark Publishers).

Nager, Norman R., and Richard H. Truitt. (1987). *Strategic Public Relations Counseling: Models from the Academy* (White Plains, NY: Longman, Inc.).

Neville, Debbie. (1999). "Creating a Press-Friendly Web Site." *Public Relations Tactics,* December.

Newman, Kelli. (2000). "The Competitive Edge of Web Site Video—Are You Ready?" *Public Relations Tactics,* June.

Paine, David. (1996). "It's Time to Put People Before Profit." *Public Relations Tactics,* December.

Pember, Don R. (1997). *Mass Media Law* (Madison, WI: Brown & Benchmark Publishers).

Petrison, Lisa A., and Paul Wang. (1993). "From Relationships to Relationship Marketing: Applying Database Technology to Public Relations," *Public Relations Review* 19, no 3.

Phipps, Kathy. (1999). "How I Became a Boss." *Public Relations Tactics,* August.

PRSA Code of Ethics—2000. (2002). <www.prsa.org/codeofethics.html>.

PRSA Web Site. (2002). Accreditation Section <www.accreditationboard.org>.

PRWEEK Web Site. (2002). <www.prweekus.com/us/index.htm>.

Restatement (Second) of Torts. (1977). Sec. 632E.

_____. (1977). Sec. 652D.

_____. (1977). Sec. 652B.

_____. (1965). Sec. 158 at 277.

Roat, Ronald, and Doug Gotthoffer. (2001). *Mass Communication on the Net* (Needham Heights, MA: Allyn & Bacon).

Seib, Philip, and Kathy Fitzpatrick. (1995). *Public Relations Ethics* (Orlando, FL: Harcourt Brace & Company).

Seitel, Fraser P. (2001). *The Practice of Public Relations* (Upper Saddle River, NJ: Prentice-Hall, Inc.).

Schmitt, Kelly. (2001). "Don't Get Clipped by Clipping Services." *Public Relations Tactics*, May.

Simon, Raymond, and Frank Winston Wylie. (1993). *Cases in Public Relations Management* (Lincolnwood, IL: NTC Business Books).

Sweeney, Katie. (2000). "SMTs are Booming, But Tougher to Book." *Public Relations Tactics*, July. Article 10, PRSA Code of Professional Standards for the Practice of Public Relations.

Thompson, M.S. (1980). *Benefit-Cost Analysis for Program Evaluation* (Beverly Hills, CA.: Sage).

Thomsen, Steven R. (1995). "Using Online Databases in Corporate Issues Management." *Public Relations Review* 21, no. 2.

VanSickle, Sharon. (1996). "The Importance of Workplace Culture in the Age of the Virtual Office." *Public Relations Tactics*, December.

Walsh, Frank. (1991). *Public Relations and the Law* (Sarasota, FL: The Institute for Public Relations Research and Education).

Wenger, Ty. (1997). "When the Sport Hits the Fan: Crisis PR in the Age of Athlete. Scandals." *Public Relations Tactics*, March.

Williams, Terrie. (1996). "The Fine Art of Saying No." *Public Relations Tactics*, October.

Wilcox, Dennis L., et al, (2001). *Essentials of Public Relations Management* (White Plains, NY: Longman, Inc.).

Witmer, Diane F. (2000). *Spinning the Web: A Handbook for Public Relations on the Internet* (New York: Addison Wesley Longman).

Index